ANDREW

Saintly
HABITS

Aquinas' 7 Simple Strategies
You Can Use to Grow in Virtue

ASCENSION
West Chester, PA

Ascension
PO Box 1990
West Chester, PA 19380
1-800-376-0520
ascensionpress.com

Cover design: Teresa Ranck

Printed in the United States of America
22 23 24 25 26 5 4 3 2 1

ISBN 978-1-954881-67-9 (paperback)
ISBN 978-1-954881-82-2 (e-book)

Contents

Introduction

The word "virtue" is not often used today. Aside from catechetical lessons that list a few virtues, or keepsakes emblazoned with the words "faith, hope, and love," we do not even hear the names of virtues. While there is still the occasional appeal to courage or justice, ethical discussion in recent years has focused more on rules and the tolerance of others' behavior. When we do hear about virtues such as chastity, sobriety, or prudence, they are often presented only from a negative perspective.

This approach to virtue, however, is in stark contrast to the attitudes of the past two and a half millennia of human history—from the mid-1800s all the way back to the sixth century BC! The truth is that whether we *speak* about virtue does not affect the *reality* of virtue. If the virtues are excellent character traits of human nature, and human nature has not changed, then the virtues we should practice have not changed—even if they are often ignored.

During the Second Vatican Council, the Church taught that we must reclaim an understanding of virtue.[1] And as recently as 1993, St. John Paul II noted the important role of virtue in his encyclical letter on truth, *Veritatis Splendor*.[2] Since then, talk of virtue, happiness, and the beatitudes has reentered moral discussion, but has not yet made its way into the wider culture.

It is no secret that our world is broken and that there is widespread unhappiness. While this is not a new phenomenon—it dates back to the sin of the first humans—it is one that past cultures and societies could better confront with the help of the virtues. Why not arm ourselves with the same weapons? Why not rediscover the secrets that enabled St. Thomas More to stand up to an unjust king and St. Lawrence, as he was being burned alive, to quip to his executioners, "Turn me over. I'm done on this side"?

1

While most of us will never face anything quite as extreme, all of us have daily struggles, some of which can, at times, seem insurmountable. If we see the height of what virtue can achieve, surely it will help with life's challenges and enable us to navigate our broken world with more grace and joy. Perhaps we will even rebuild some small part of it, even if that is ourselves.

This book was written not to revive an old intellectual concept, but so that we can be transformed. It was written not only to reclaim an understanding of virtue, but to develop a life of virtue.

1

Fake It Till You Make It

Ads for weight-loss diets abound, promising amazing results such as losing twenty pounds in thirty days. Some clients will experience this level of success ... only to gain the weight back and have to start a new diet the next year.

Those who need to endure a lengthy commute know from experience full well that an insufferable number of red lights, construction projects, inattentive drivers, and car accidents are going to slow them down. Yet somehow these occurrences still raise one's blood pressure and spark the need for another cup of coffee.

For several years, I was one of these impatient drivers, commuting every day to Washington, DC from suburban Maryland. It was a long drive, with many red lights and stop signs. I thought (incorrectly) that I could make the drive quicker than was physically possible, which of course led to frustration. After years of this commute, I expected that I would have accepted it and become patient. After all, I had made the drive so many times! But something was still lacking if I were to have a peaceful commute.

Whether or not we have experienced fad diets or rush hour traffic, all of us have the made mistakes about things we do all the time. We might even make the same mistake all the time. When we were children, we were taught that "practice makes perfect." But if we practice the same activities, day in and day out, why do we never seem to reach "perfect"?

When we strive to grow in moderation, patience, or any other virtue, it can be deflating when we seem to be making no progress or when we find ourselves failing at a virtue that we thought we already had. How is it that we can practice a virtue over and over but still fall short? The answer is that mere practice is only half of what is need to grow in virtue, but to understand the other half we need to look a little closer at what a virtue really is. This chapter, in the course of recommending the first strategy for growing in virtue, will explain the fundamentals of what a virtue is and is not.

The Strategy

I am good at *starting* workout regimens, less so at following through with them. I typically start with light weights to ease my way into the routine of working out, planning to eventually increase the weight. The problem is that I have to do so many repetitions with the lighter weights that I get bored and do not want to find the time for it. As a result, my muscles never really get stronger from such a workout. At best, they maintain their level of strength. Ironically, my muscle building does not seem to come from weight training but from picking up my children as they grow bigger. Their continual growth forces me to exert myself more and more as I toss them in the air or lift them to high places.

If a person lifts a ten-pound weight ten times every day, he may keep his muscle strength consistent, but he will not increase his strength. To really become stronger, he will need to increase the weight that he lifts or the number of times that he lifts it. He needs to push his muscles beyond their current level to increase their strength. If he works his way up to lifting a fifty-pound weight, but then over time decreases the weight that he lifts, his strength will diminish because his exercise does not meet the level of his strength. The key to strengthening the muscle is to increase the intensity of the workout. So I will need to establish a consistent workout routine before my kids grow too big for me to lift them!

The same is true for the virtues. To develop a particular virtue, one must act beyond the "level" or "strength" of his habit. If he simply performs the same type of act with the same level of intensity, even if he does so a thousand times, his virtue will not increase. He must act with greater intensity. The way to become generous is to act more generous than you already are; the way to become courageous is to act more courageous than you actually are; and the way to become temperate is to act more temperate than you actually are.

In time, the greater level of generosity, courage, or temperance you are "acting" will become your true character—and you will have to act even more generous, courageous, or temperate to keep growing in these virtues! If you start to slacken, however, and act with lesser generosity, courage, or temperance, then your virtue will weaken. It could even become a vice, just as a muscle can weaken when a weight trainer uses lighter weights or stops lifting altogether.

For this reason, I call the first strategy for growing in virtue *"fake it till you make it."* There is a paradox here: the only way to become virtuous is to act virtuous even though you are not yet virtuous, and the only way to grow further in virtue is to act more virtuous than you already are.

But am I not acting in a way that is not true to my character? Doesn't this make me a hypocrite? Rest easy. A hypocrite is someone who wants to give the *appearance* of having a certain trait but does not actually have the trait and has no desire to acquire it. One who is striving to live a specific virtue, on the other hand, does desire to acquire it. He imitates it until it becomes his (more on this in chapter seven).

This is no different from how young athletes imitate the professionals to acquire their skills. But the number of times a person does a good thing does not make a difference if he or she is just "going through the motions." Why not? To understand this strategy, let's look more closely at what a virtue is.

What Is a Virtue?

We hear many platitudes about virtues—"Patience is a virtue"; "Virtue is its own reward"—but do we know what a virtue actually is? Often, we talk about virtues as if they are things we can collect: "She has great patience." "He has a lot of courage." We understand what someone means by these phrases, but

[handwritten marginal note:] To be a better man, I must be a different man. Ex.: "I've changed." "I'm not who I was."

this way of speaking about virtues can lead to simple misunderstandings, which in turn can lead to disappointment regarding our moral progress. Virtues are not "things" we can collect, like figurines or trading cards. A surgeon never operated on a patient and said, "Aha! I see the problem. Mr. Smith is missing a 'justice.' We will have to get him a transplant of one STAT!"

It may seem like a small matter, but it is more accurate to say "she is patient" than "she has patience," and "he is courageous" rather than "he has courage." This is because a virtue is not an external "thing" that one acquires but rather a description of one's interior character, which shows itself through action. Thinking of a virtue as a "thing" can lead us to the false idea that once a virtue is obtained, we possess it forever, just like something we buy.

A virtue, however, is a character trait, something that can develop or diminish. Therefore, we need to give it constant attention to preserve and grow in it. Things that we own can be tucked away in the attic and forgotten, but we still possess them. A virtue that we forget and stop practicing disappears (in fact, it does not just disappear but is replaced—as we will see in the next chapter).

If we want to have any hope of attaining a virtue, we need to first understand what a virtue is. Like a person going on a scavenger hunt, if we do not know what we are looking for, how can we ever find it? A virtue is not just any character trait, however; it is always a *good* character trait. Philosophically, a virtue can be defined as a habit of performing good actions that makes the one who possesses it good. What does this mean?

Virtue Is a Habit

Here, we need to clarify what we mean by "habit." When we use the word "habit" in our everyday speech, we usually mean something different from what the word originally meant and how it is used in moral philosophy.

Today, when we speak of "habits," we usually refer to bad habits—things such as biting your nails or forgetting to turn off the oven. My personal bad habit is locking the car three times in a row. These are all mindless activities, things we generally are not even aware of doing until someone brings them to our attention (or we discover that the oven is on fire). I know full well that my car doors do not get any more locked after the second or third click, but that does not stop me from clicking the remote three times. These bad habits are things we just do. After a while we might feel off if we do not do them, but that is only because we have become so accustomed to doing them. But we could have just as easily become accustomed to lock the car five times rather than three times, to bite our lip rather than our nails, or to leave the bathroom light on rather than the oven.

These sorts of habits are easy to eliminate if we put our mind to it. We might need to use sticky notes or ask a friend to remind us, but once we are able to focus on our actions we can choose to act differently. As weird as it may feel to me to lock the car just once, it does not take much effort for me to do it. A 2010 study concluded that these types of habits can be formed or replaced simply by doing the same action every day for sixty-six days.[3] Similarly, a 2015 study claims that a person can develop a habit of exercising by making sure to exercise four times a week for six weeks.[4] In the case of such habits, making or breaking them is not just a matter of time and commitment but repeated action.

When it comes to virtues, the word "habit" derives from the Latin *habitus*, which means "something that is held." This is why we call what a consecrated religious wears a "habit." A habit is what our character "wears"—it is something that is second nature to us.

Habits Versus Dispositions

If a virtue is not a habit in the way we think of habits today, how exactly do we develop the right kind of habits—the virtuous kind? As the strategy of this chapter shows, it is not automatic and takes hard work. One act, or even a handful of repeated acts, will not develop a habit. They will, however, develop a *disposition*, and a disposition is a first step on the way to a virtuous habit. But what is a disposition, and how is it different from a virtuous habit?

A disposition simply inclines or leads us toward some action. In other words, due to the prior choices we have made, we are simply more likely to keep making those same choices. Any action we take disposes us to act in a similar manner, simply because it is easier to do something we are familiar with than to do something new and untried.

We can see this in our own choices. When we first learn a route to get to work, we are more likely to take that same route the next time than to find another. When we tell a lie, we find that it is that much easier to tell another. When we get a good night's rest, we are likely to try to do it again.

These dispositions, however, are simply that—inclinations. They make us more likely to do something, but in no way do they force or determine us to choose certain acts. It is just about as easy for a driver to find a new route to work, for a person who lied once to tell the truth, or for a person who got a good night's sleep to stay up too late the next night. What primarily differentiates a disposition from a habit is it is easy to change.

Over time, if we consistently choose to act in accordance with a disposition, it can develop into a habit. A habit is a true character trait that is difficult to change, so it is more enduring than a disposition. While it is still possible to change a habit, it will take quite a bit of intentional effort. We have all heard the expression "old habits die hard." When we describe what a person is like (for example, "he is studious" or "she is courteous"), we are describing his or her habits. Habits become so engrained in our behavior that they become "second nature" to us.

Here is an analogy that helps illustrate the difference between a habit and a disposition. When I was young, I was a Boy Scout, and I still love to hike forest trails. I find walking through nature to be very soothing, and it is exciting to me to discover strange natural formations of rocks, cliffs, or streams. It can be fun to go off the trail to observe something or to make a shortcut, but this can also be a bit risky. If you are not good at finding your bearings, you can easily get turned around or lost. For these reasons, I usually stick to the marked and well-worn paths (although sometimes blazing a new trail is necessary when I encounter a fallen tree or flooding).

Habit formation is somewhat like hiking in the woods. Imagine you are taking a walk and come to the edge of a dense forest. You want to walk through the forest to the other side but cannot find any path. The only way to get through is to make your own. The next day, you come back to the same forest. You want to get to the other side again, and since there is still no clear path, it would be just as easy for you to blaze a new trail as on the previous day. But you do happen to notice a few broken branches and some underbrush bent over from yesterday's path. You figure that your path worked yesterday, so you might as well take it again. You are a little more comfortable with it than with the uncertainty of making a new path. So, you take your path again, and you take it again the next day, and you continue taking it day after day.

Over time, the path becomes increasingly more defined. The low-hanging branches are cleared out and the grass has worn down to hard dirt. It is easy to find your way, and you are confident that it will get you where you want to go. On occasion, you may feel adventurous and try to chart a new path, but you come back to the well-worn path since it is more familiar and convenient. New paths take more work and can be uncomfortable. If for some reason you decide that you need to make a new path—perhaps because you think you could find a shorter way or a more beautifully scenic route—you are free to do so, though this usually takes a lot of effort and determination to stick to it. You really would *want* to take this path.

In this analogy, the hard-worn path represents our habits, while the paths we may take from time to time represent our dispositions. Until we have developed a habit, we are likely to act in a variety of ways, becoming disposed to this act and then to that act, one act and then another act. But over time we become more comfortable with certain acts—we find them to be easier, more efficient, more enjoyable. They become our default choices; we reliably choose them—so reliably, in fact, that others come to expect them of us. They would describe us by these reliable acts, whether they are acts of generosity, joyfulness, cowardice, wittiness, rage, stubbornness, or gentleness. We could, of course, change these habits—just as we can blaze a new path through the forest and make it well-worn—but it will take serious commitment.

Why would we want to change our habits, though, if we find them to be comfortable and easy? The only reason is if we become convinced that they are not as comfortable, enjoyable, or efficient as we first thought. Like coming to a fallen tree or flooded stream in the forest, maybe we find that our current path no longer works. This brings us to the next part of the definition of a virtue.

Virtue Does Good

Recall our definition of virtue—a habit of performing good actions that makes its possessor good. We have looked at what it means to call a virtue a habit. When we did so, you may have noticed that some of the character traits listed were desirable (generosity, joyfulness, wittiness) while others were not (cowardice, rage, stubbornness). A habit is simply an engrained pattern of behavior, but that behavior can be good or evil.

To put it another way, as humans, we are made for certain activities that distinguish us from things like animals and plants, and which perfect us as human beings. We naturally desire to love and be loved within a family, to make friendships and pursue goals within society, to keep ourselves healthy and safe, to acquire knowledge, and to worship something (hopefully, God!). Some activities help us to achieve these goals; these actions befit our nature, and so we call them good. Other activities work against these goals; they are opposed to our nature, and so we call them evil.

When we choose the good, we become more excellent humans and experience fulfillment since we act according to our nature. When we choose evil, we act less-than-human and ultimately become frustrated because we act like something beneath us. We can, then, consistently choose behavior that is good and thus develop good habits, or consistently choose behavior that is harmful to us and thus develop bad habits. We call the former virtues and the latter vices.

As we have seen, a virtue is a good habit; it is a character trait that befits our human nature because it helps us to flourish and achieve truly human goals with excellence. A vice is a bad habit; it is a character trait that wounds our human nature and impedes us from achieving truly human goals well. (We will look more closely at vices in the next chapter.)

But what about the last part of the definition of virtue? How does virtue make its possessor good? This part of the definition is important because if our habits are not making us into good people, then the endeavor is worthless. If our habits are not making us good, then we are not acting with enough intensity to actually grow in virtue.

Virtue Is a "Good-Making" Character Trait

To say that a virtue makes its possessor good may, at first glance, seem redundant. If a virtue is a habit of doing the good, wouldn't this automatically make the person with a virtue good? Unfortunately, it is not quite that simple. There are three different ways that we can do good things, sometimes even routinely, without them making us into more moral people. While these three ways are not necessarily immoral, nevertheless they do not lead us to virtue. For that reason, we need to be aware of them in order to make sure we do not fall into them, but rather focus our efforts on what will produce true virtue.

First, there are times when we might do something good simply by chance or coincidence. While the consequences of our action may be good, we did not perform it in order to achieve these effects. This could be because we did not know these effects were possible, or because we did not want to bring about these effects at this time, or because we did not desire to bring about these effects ... or for any number of other reasons. The point is that we acted with some ignorance of the situation's circumstances, and therefore we did not fully choose the action that we performed.

This is what we call an involuntary act. In Latin, the word *voluntas* means "will." To act involuntarily is therefore to act against one's will, either because we did not want to perform the action or because we simply did not willfully choose it. We might have been under duress, or we might have been ignorant of the circumstances. An involuntary act cannot be a fully moral act because it does not follow from what makes us human—namely, our ability to reason and to make free choices. This is why we do not (or at least should not) blame people for making mistakes, and why we do not confess mistakes in the sacrament of Reconciliation. They are involuntary, and thus they are not blameworthy (or praiseworthy if they are a happy accident). We might blame prior negligence that leads to the accident, but this is because negligence could be a voluntary act and therefore flow from our reasoning and choice. An accident, however, insofar as it is involuntary, is not a blameworthy or praiseworthy action.

A virtue, then, must be developed through voluntary acts—that is, through actions that we deliberately choose for some intended purpose. Things that happen by chance do not fit this criterion, and so they are unable to build true virtue.

Wildcat!

A story based on one I heard from an old acquaintance will illustrate the point. A man, let's call him Phil, was traveling through an unfamiliar part of the country. He missed a turn, and as night came on, he became hopelessly lost on winding backroads through a forested area, where the only light came from the front doors of occasional houses. He was desperate to get back to the main road.

Suddenly, a shadow descended on the road, and the car came to a crashing halt. Phil waited to catch his breath, then left his car to inspect what he had hit. At the same time, people from the surrounding houses, who had heard both the crash and a screeching yelp, cautiously peered out their windows, only to then come out of their doors and into the street, cheering. To his great surprise, Phil found a dead wildcat in front of his car and was soon informed by the neighbors that this wildcat had been terrorizing their town. They hailed him as a hero, but he was simply relieved that they could give him directions to get back to the main road and on his way again.

In the story, the locals praised the driver as a courageous hero for saving them from the wildcat. It is true that Phil killed the animal and therefore saved the town, which is a great thing and worthy of celebration. However, this was not Phil's intention. He was completely unaware of where he was, let alone that there was a predator on the prowl, and simply wanted to get back to the main road. The killing of the wildcat was an involuntary act, an accident. It would have been a different scenario if Phil knew about the wildcat and was intentionally patrolling the road in search of it, hoping to bring peace to the community. This would have been a voluntary act, something thought through and willed, and could have been truly courageous and praiseworthy. As the story goes, however, saving the town was an accident, and Phil did not suddenly become a courageous person because of it.

An involuntary act, then, is something that is not deliberately chosen, so it is not fully moral and cannot make us virtuous. For an act to be truly virtuous, it must be chosen because the person sees the good in it and desires that good.

Custom and Routine

There is a second way in which we might do something good that does not make us good (that is, moral), and that is when we act out of custom, routine, or tradition. Customs and routines are things we choose to follow—they are voluntary—but they differ from virtuous actions because we approach them differently on the part of our reasoning.

Take some time to ask the people you know why they follow the customs and traditions that they do. You can even pose the question to yourself. Most of the time people will respond by saying that they do not know why or will respond with some vague understanding that the action is good.

Why do you always go to bed early and wake up early? That is how I was raised. Why do you take your hat off when you step inside a building? It is polite. Why do you bless yourself when you drive by a church? It is what my grandmother always did. Why do you eat turkey for Thanksgiving? It is what we do in America!

You will probably receive similar answers when asking people this sort of question. The answers typically are not very profound. They can often boil down to "I do it because that is what you do!" To be clear, the argument here is not that customs and traditions are bad, or that we should abandon them if we do not understand them. There is something to be said for maintaining traditions, despite our lack of understanding of their meaning. But there is something even greater to be said for learning and understanding why we keep the routines and traditions that we do, so that we can either have greater respect for them and derive greater joy from them if they are good or abandon them if they are irrational and harmful.

Growing up, my family had a tradition of buying sweet bread for Easter morning. I never understood why we got the bread or why we only got it at Easter—I just knew that "that is what you do at Easter" and it tasted good. Many years later, I learned that the bread symbolizes the risen Christ, and the egg in it symbolizes new life (which we have through Christ). This knowledge added to the meaning of the tradition and enabled me to participate in it more willfully. On the other hand, after years of Thanksgiving meals together, at one point my extended family came to the realization that no one actually enjoyed eating turkey, and we were only serving it because "that is what you do" at Thanksgiving. The following year, we switched to ham. Traditions are easy to change if they are not grounded in a rational choice or if the good reason has been lost or forgotten.

Custom and routine can certainly be a good starting point for developing virtue. If you are already used to doing a good thing, then you are halfway there! But doing a good thing in itself does not necessarily make you a good person, even if you do it routinely. If the necessary intensity is lacking, a virtue will not develop. In the case of custom, it is our lack of understanding why the action is good that prevents it from being intense enough. A true virtue will entail not only free choice but also understanding of *why* that choice is good.

For example, you may have heard of the term "cultural Catholic." This label is often applied to people who were raised in the Catholic Faith and maintain many of its traditions (such as hanging a crucifix over a doorway, having a picture of the pope on the wall, putting up a Christmas tree, perhaps even abstaining from eating meat on Fridays) but otherwise do not understand the Church's teachings or allow them to impact their daily lives and choices in a significant way. Such a person may attend Mass on Christmas and Easter (because "that is what we do as Catholics") but not on any other Sunday. Going to Mass on Christmas and Easter is certainly a good thing, but if one really understands *why* it was a good thing, he would attend Mass every Sunday.

Custom is a good starting point, but until one understands why an action is good, it does not have any transformative power over his moral choices. The transition from doing something because it is "what we always have done" to recognizing that this action is the fulfillment of some part of our nature to worship God and offer thanks for his great works is what allows for the transition from custom to virtue. By understanding the goodness of the act, we are then able to let that understanding shape and inform our moral choices—and to unite these choices into a coherent and consistent character.

It should also be noted that we can follow a custom or tradition that is good but for the wrong reasons, which will obviously prevent us from becoming morally good. To continue with the example of only attending Mass on Christmas and Easter, a person might do so because that is what his family always does—and he cannot wait to make fun of it afterward at dinner! This person does a good thing (attends Mass) but for a bad reason (to mock the Faith). Clearly, then, this custom does not make him virtuous. (We will consider this concept of "false virtue" in chapter five.)

By this point, we have noted how matters of chance are not virtuous, because the person performing them lacks full understanding of the situation and lacks a voluntary choice of the action. We have also seen that custom is not the same as virtue. From this discussion we can see why it is so important that we both act voluntarily and understand why our actions are good in order to grow in virtue. Without these two elements, we can never hope to act with the level of intensity necessary to attain a virtue.

There is, however, one final category of action that falls short of true moral virtue. It is a type of activity that contains these two necessary elements but does not make good use of them. While it is still a type of human excellence, it does not make us morally good. For those of us reading books on morality, it can be a temptation to be satisfied with the knowledge of good and evil but to not act on it. In other words, we may develop an intellectual virtue that does not lead to moral virtue. Let's see how these types of virtue differ.

Intellectual and Moral Virtues

If chance lacks understanding and free choice, and custom lacks understanding but has free choice, could there be a third category of action that has understanding but lacks free choice? Since someone who has understanding always makes free choices, we can better describe this third category as understanding the goodness or badness of actions but not using that knowledge and understanding to actually live well. This is possible in a person who possesses vice, that is, a "vicious" person.

We will look at vice more closely in the next two chapters. The point here is to show how one can possess what is called intellectual virtue and still be "vicious"—that is, acting according to a vice—whereas one who possesses moral virtue cannot possibly be vicious. This distinction will be helpful for our strategy because it will show us that, while knowledge is very important for virtue formation, it is not the only thing that matters. In addition to getting our reasoning straight, we also need to will and perform the right activities so that the intensity of our habits increases.

As we have seen, a virtue is a type of perfection of our human capabilities. Since we can think and choose, we can also perfect these abilities. Perfections of our thinking abilities are called intellectual virtues, and these include prudence, wisdom, understanding, knowledge (everything from biology to astronomy to economics), and various skills (everything from knitting to athletics to cooking). These are all truly virtues inasmuch as they are perfections of our intellect. We would all rather have knowledge than ignorance, and it is obvious that having knowledge or wisdom about certain things makes us better able to make good use of them.

Intellectual virtues are rightly called virtues because they are perfections of our intellect, but they technically fall short of the full sense of a virtue. Why? While these virtues allow us to do good things—such as make correct mathematical calculations, comprehend reading material, or create beautiful art—they do not necessarily make us into good people. To put it another way, intellectual virtues present us with the ability or opportunity to do good things, but not the right use of this ability. We could define them as "habits of knowing and understanding truth" rather than "habits of performing good actions that make their possessor good."

Certainly, intellectual virtues can be a great boon when we want to do good things. The better a person understands biology, the better she can care for a person who is unwell. The better a person understands mathematics and economic philosophy, the better he can make generous and worthwhile donations to good causes. Yet, it is certainly not the case that this knowledge is necessary for doing good. We need only to look to young children to see how a person can be so caring and generous with very little knowledge. How often do we encounter brilliant people who are arrogant and selfish, while we meet less educated people who are warm and hospitable?

The classic caricature is the mad scientist who knows all the mysteries of science but puts that knowledge to evil ends by creating instruments of torture and death. We may think of the classic line by Dr. Ian Malcolm in the film *Jurassic Park* as he chastises the park owner, saying, "Your scientists were so preoccupied with whether or not they *could* that they didn't stop to think if they *should*."

To become good, moral people, the perfections of character that we need to focus on are the moral virtues. These are the perfections of our capacities to choose and to express emotions, which not only allow us to do good things but also make us into better people.

Keep Up the Intensity

But this brings us back full circle to the dilemma at the beginning of the chapter: Why we do not always see ourselves becoming better persons though we do good things? As we have seen, half of the answer is that if our good acts are just occasional occurrences—and thereby they only form dispositions—or if they are by chance, nonreflective customs, or exclusively intellectual perfections, then they cannot make us better people. Something is still missing.

Thinking back to our analogy with weight training, we are reminded of the missing factor—intensity. So often we focus on the quantity of our actions but do not pay attention to the quality of our actions. We focus on how often we repeat an activity, but we do not think about how intensely we do it.

The first secret to growing in virtue is to understand that the *quantity* of our good actions is less important than their *quality*. In fact, the repetition of good actions is only important insofar as it gives us ample opportunities to perform them with greater intensity. While a true virtue is a habit of performing good acts, this habit only gains its strength and stability from the intensity of our prior acts. If we only ever do good things in shallow or unthinking ways—that is, with minimal intensity—then we will only ever form dispositions for performing good actions. We will never form habits of performing good actions—and virtue is a habit, not merely a disposition.

How To

Practically speaking, how does one act with greater intensity to grow in virtue? There are various ways. As we will see in chapter three, one way to act with greater intensity is to better understand better good actions are actually good. This is like knowing which muscles you are working on when you lift certain weights and do certain exercises. If you know what muscle is being built, you can focus on having the right posture and ensuring that the correct muscle is being challenged, rather than letting other muscles compensate for it. Likewise, if we understand why a virtuous act is good, we will not let mindless routine compensate for the virtue we are striving for; our understanding will keep us acting intentionally and deliberately, and thereby with greater intensity.

A different approach to acting with greater intensity is to set small goals for ourselves. Strictly speaking, while virtue cannot be quantified, we can have some idea of when we act with more or less virtue. If we want to grow in generosity, we can set goals of helping more and more people during the week, or of performing bigger favors than usual. If we want to grow in temperance, we can set goals of incrementally eating healthier. By setting such goals, we make sure that we do not become complacent and hit a plateau on the ascent toward virtue. Instead, we will continuously increase the intensity of our virtues.

So practice does indeed make perfect, but it must be true and intense practice. True attainment and increase in virtue come through striving beyond one's dispositions, striving for the good with greater intensity. And therefore the repetition of good acts is important—because the more we practice a good action, the more opportunities we have to increase in intensity.

Let's face it: growing in virtue is hard. But so is building stronger muscles. And developing sports skills. And becoming a musical virtuoso. Anything worth doing in life is difficult, and pursuing virtue is the most worthwhile because it makes all our other endeavors and relationships easier.

Now that we see the main requirement that makes virtue possible, how do we best strive for this greater intensity? To answer that question, we now turn to the next strategy.

Strategies

1. **Fake it till you make it** – Repeat good acts with intensity. Quality is more important than quantity.

2

Overshooting the Target

Cornhole is a lawn game that has swept the nation in recent years. It involves two players (or teams) standing ten or twelve feet across from each other and taking turns attempting to toss bean bags onto platforms. These platforms are propped up at an angle, and while a player may earn a point for landing the bean bag on the board, he will receive more points for getting the bean bag into a hole in the board. As with most popular outdoor games, it is easy to learn but difficult to master, and perhaps the most challenging aspect is learning precisely how hard to toss the bean bag so that you neither fall short of the target nor overshoot.

I remember that when I first learned to play the game, the targets seemed close together and I was worried about tossing the bean bag too far. As it turned out, I kept falling short of the target almost every throw. I knew I needed to give the bag a stronger toss, but I was so worried about overshooting that I would never give it enough force and kept falling short. Eventually, I needed to convince myself to toss the bean bag hard enough that it felt like I would overshoot it, because this was, in fact, the appropriate amount of force necessary to land on the board. Since I was naturally falling short of the target, I had to aim to overshoot the target in order to actually reach it. Since I was so worried of overshooting, I never actually did—the fear was self-limiting in that respect. But when I threw in a way that felt like overshooting, I managed to hit the target. In time, what once felt like overshooting began to feel normal, and I developed a more correct sense for how hard I should throw the bean bag.

This illustration will help to explain the second strategy for growing in virtue: *overshooting the target*. There are many parallels between games of accuracy and virtue, as a virtue is the target we aim for and vices are the deficiencies (underthrows) or excesses (overthrows) of that target. This chapter, in explaining its strategy, will focus on the difference between a virtue and a vice and how the perspectives of the virtuous and vicious person differ. This strategy is all about correcting our misperceptions about what is virtuous, and so studying these perspectives will help us to better use the strategy.

Evil

While the previous chapter presented a general overview of virtues and vices, it is worth reviewing some of the more important details for this second strategy to grow in virtue. Recall that a virtue is a habit of performing good actions that makes its possessor good. We noted that developing a virtue requires some understanding of what actions are good and free choice of those actions, and that, in time, virtues become descriptions of our character. They become a "second nature" to us. Virtues thus make us into better, more excellent humans because they give us the freedom to act according to our human nature as God designed it and to perfect it.

A vice is the opposite of a virtue. It is a habit of performing evil actions that makes its possessor evil.

Since we have used the "E" word, we need to make an important clarification. It may seem harsh to call certain vices evil. For example, while almost everyone acknowledges that hatred is evil, what about cowardice? Does it really make a person evil if he has an irrational fear of clowns? By coming to a better understanding of what evil is, we will better understand just how detrimental vices are for our growth in virtue. We will also better understand why there are at least two vices for every virtue and how the target we are aiming for rests somewhere in between them.

We should note there are two different types of evil—*physical evil* and *moral evil*. When we hear the word "evil," we typically think of moral evil, which are actions performed against God's law that make one a bad person. But there is also physical evil. For example, when a hurricane destroys thousands of homes and kills hundreds of people, this is an evil for those who suffer from this event. When a lion kills and eats a gazelle, this is an evil for the gazelle. When a virus infects a person, this is an evil for that person. However, we would not call the hurricane, the lion, or the virus *immoral*. They are not free, moral agents that have control over their actions, such that the hurricane could agree to stay over the ocean, the lion could decide to become a vegetarian, or the virus could try to live as a good bacterium. In fact, what each of these things did was "good" in that they each followed their respective natures as a hurricane, lion, or virus.

To call a person or thing evil, then, is to say that it causes itself or another person or thing to experience something that is against its nature. The gazelle suffers evil from the lion because it strives to live, not to be eaten. The human suffers evil from the hurricane or virus because she strives to have shelter and maintain good health, not to be killed. Evil is simply that which harms or wounds one's nature.

Physical evil is suffered passively, while moral evil is actively chosen. But both are harmful; both are evil. Thus, to have an irrational fear of clowns is evil for a person because that person has not been made by God to have such an irrational fear. As long as the person possesses this fear, he is not living the most excellent human life; he still has room for greater human perfection. This does not mean that he sins by being afraid of clowns. He may just try to avoid clowns as much as possible. However, this irrational fear could be the occasion for sin. Imagine if he were to attack or demonize a clown out of fear, or to fail to fulfill some important obligation because there was a clown in the near vicinity. Proper courage in the face of clowns, however, could never be the occasion for sin. Why not? Because courage, as a virtue, is a "good-making" character trait, and sin does not make us good.

The point is that all vices are *evil*, but not all vices are *sinful*. Still, all vices can be an occasion of sin since they are moral weaknesses and failings—and some vices are always sinful, such as dishonesty or idolatry. To call a vice evil is simply to acknowledge that it is not the perfection of human living and is an area that needs correction for the individual to experience true happiness.

A virtue perfects our nature while a vice wounds our nature. A virtue can never be the occasion of sin (although in chapter five we will see how some vices can give the appearance of being a virtue), while a vice can always at least potentially lead one to sin. Thus, it is important to identify and eliminate any vices that we may possess in order to grow in true virtue.

Finding the Mean-ing

How exactly do we identify a vice? In general, if a virtue is a perfection of human character, then a vice is simply any imperfection of character. To be more precise, we can return to the cornhole analogy. If the perfection of playing cornhole is to hit the target, the imperfections are to undershoot (toss the beanbag with deficient force) or overshoot (toss it with excessive force). Likewise, a vice is some deficiency or excess of a virtue. But a deficiency or excess of what?

In the first chapter, we saw that to perform a virtuous act one must know what actions are good and then choose them. It is not virtuous to accidentally do something good, nor is it virtuous to know what should be done but not do it. Both knowledge and action are required, but the knowledge of what is good directs our actions. So, we can describe a virtue as right reason applied to action—and the action becomes good as long as it follows from right reasoning about what is good.

Therefore, when we speak of vices as deficiencies or excesses, we mean that they are deficiencies or excesses of right reason about how we should act. A vice of deficiency does not quite meet the consideration of what is reasonable, while a vice of excess goes beyond the bounds of what is reasonable.

Let's take the virtue of courage as an example here. Courage, also called fortitude, is the character trait that helps us to reasonably manage our emotions of fear and aggression, making sure that our fears do not prevent us from doing what is right and good, and that our aggression does not spur us on to do something foolish. If our fear does overcome us and prevent us from doing what is good on a regular basis, then that deficiency of reason (seeing the situation correctly) makes us cowardly. However, if we lack a reasonable amount of fear, that excess of aggression causes us to act beyond what is reasonable and become foolhardy.

One summer, I opened my garage door to find a large rat snake. Rat snakes are not venomous, but they can bite. Once I got over the initial shock of the snake invading my home, I assessed the situation. I have no formal training in dealing with pests, but neither is this type of snake a major threat. Had I run screaming from the garage and put off the yardwork I was going to do until the snake left, I would have acted cowardly. Even if the snake stayed put, there was enough space in the garage that I could still get around it to what I needed, so there was no reason to let my fear get the best of me. On the other hand, if I had walked over and tried to pick up the snake and throw it into the woods with my bare hands, I would have been foolhardy, since I do not know how to properly grab or carry a snake. If I managed to do this successfully it would be out of sheer luck. Instead, I studied the snake and its movements for a bit, approached it from behind, and hit it with the edge of a shovel, dealing a mortal wound.

It was not that I had no fear of the snake. After all, courage does not eliminate fear but simply prevents our fear from causing us to flee from what is good—in this case getting my yard work done. It is the foolish person who has no fear. Instead, I moderated my reasonable fear of the snake, came up with the safest way to remove this obstacle, and acted on it.

The point of the example is to show that we can conceptualize virtue as situated between two opposite vices, one of deficiency (falling short of what is reasonable) and the other of excess (going beyond what is reasonable). The philosophical term for how a virtue is related to its opposite vices is that a virtue is a *mean* between the two extremes of deficiency and excess.

The use of the word "mean" here is similar to how it is used in mathematics to describe an average of a range of numbers. Similarly, a virtue is a sort of midpoint between two opposite extremes of reason. However, a virtue is not always a mathematical midpoint equally between the two vices.

Vicious but Not Equal

It is not always the case that each vice is equally unreasonable. While both vices are moral imperfections and can lead to sin, some are worse than others because they are naturally further from right reason.

For example, cowardice, which is a defect, is more opposed to courage than foolhardiness, which is an excess. Why? Because one already needs to moderate his fear somewhat to be foolhardy. This explains why foolhardy people are sometimes (wrongfully) praised, but cowardly people are never praised. Had I picked up the snake with my bare hands and thrown it into the woods, my family or neighbors may have praised me for being courageous, when in fact I was not. Foolhardiness, because it is closer to courage, can look like courage if the person gets lucky—however, if the snake bit me and I dropped it to go to the hospital, no one would praise me for courage but would instead judge the action for what it truly was—foolhardiness.

To take another example, lust (an excess) is more opposed to chastity than prudishness (a defect) because prudishness restrains irrational desire, even if too much, while lust does not restrain it. Chastity is the virtue of expressing our love well to others. It helps us to not only restrain sexual desire that is unreasonable, but also to make sure that we actively show affection in appropriate ways depending on the relationship and circumstances. In most relationships and circumstances, the affection due to others is somewhat reserved: holding hands, hugging, a peck on the cheek. For this reason, the prudish person who rarely if ever hugs or kisses may (wrongly) appear chaste, while the person who cannot control his urges and is always looking for ways to have sex is clearly lustful. While prudishness is closer to chastity than lust, it is still not virtuous because it is deficient in reasonable expressions of love and affection.

Circumstances

Additionally, unlike the mathematical mean, the virtuous mean is dependent on the given circumstances. While the mean of 1, 3, and 5 will always be 3 in all times and places, the virtuous mean of an action is somewhat conditional. As if it weren't already hard enough, when it comes to virtue, we need to hit a moving target!

For example, what is courageous in one situation may not be what is courageous in another situation. It may be virtuous for a fully trained firefighter with the right equipment to enter a burning building, but it would be foolhardy for an untrained man with no equipment and bad asthma to run into a burning building. (As mentioned, since foolhardiness is closer to courage than cowardice, this may be mistaken for true courage, though—more on this in chapter five). To take another example, it may be virtuous to express righteous anger at someone who pushes an elderly lady, but it would be excessive to express the same degree of anger toward someone who playfully pushes you in a game of tag.

Therefore, the reasonable, virtuous response in any situation depends on the given circumstances. This means that the truly virtuous act encompasses both objective and subjective dimensions. In other words, some actions will always be wrong, but for other actions, what is right depends on the circumstances.

The Cardinal Virtues

By this point, we see how a virtue is a midpoint between two extremes opposed to right reason. These extremes, called vices, impede our ability to live full, and fully happy, human lives. Our goal is to reach that virtuous midpoint, but what is reasonable in a given situation can shift slightly (within objective parameters) due to the given circumstances. We are close to being able to explain fully this chapter's strategy for growing in virtue and attaining this midpoint, but before we do so it will be helpful to define and explain some of these virtues and vices. After all, if we are aiming for a target, we need to know what the target is! By reflecting on some of the main virtues and their opposing vices, we will be better able to identify when we are overshooting or undershooting the target, and how much we need to adjust our approach.

At this point in the book, we have named many virtues and vices, and what we called a virtue or vice may, in some cases, have been surprising.

How many virtues are there? St. Thomas Aquinas describes at least forty-four in his works. As for vices, there are at least two for every virtue (since we can err in reason by deficiency or excess), but sometimes there is more than one way that we can err by deficiency or excess, resulting in even more vices!

If reflecting on some 150 virtues and vices sounds daunting, never fear. Fortunately, we do not have to examine each one. The Christian tradition has always recognized seven virtues to be the most important. Three of these virtues (faith, hope, and charity) are exclusive to Christians because they require sanctifying grace, and they will be covered in chapter six. The remaining four virtues (prudence, justice, fortitude, and temperance) are called the "cardinal virtues" (from the Latin word *cardo,* "hinge"). These four have been emphasized among the entire range of virtues because the entire moral life hinges on them.

In other words, a person cannot be truly moral if he lacks one of these four virtues, and every act of virtue will have some aspect of each one of these virtues. All other virtues are merely specifications of prudence, justice, fortitude, or temperance, or they are what we could call sub-virtues. Thus, in looking at these four virtues, we have, in a way, looked at all the virtues. In the following pages we will look more closely at these virtues, their corresponding vices, and a few of the more important sub-virtues. This will give us a clear picture of the dynamism of the virtuous life and the targets we need to aim for. If we can find where we are overshooting or undershooting, we can recalibrate accordingly to hit that sweet spot.

Prudence

Prudence typically heads off the list of the cardinal virtues because it is the virtue concerned with right reason. We need right reason in order to act by any virtue. Sometimes called "practical wisdom," prudence is the virtue that identifies precisely what the virtuous mean of action is in a particular situation so that we can perform a good act and avoid sin and vice. Prudence fulfills an indispensable role in the moral life: without prudence, it is not possible to possess any virtue, precisely because prudence is what allows us to accurately determine how we should act. In other words, prudence is the virtue that helps us to see the target clearly and to know precisely how much effort to use in pursuing it. If it were cornhole, prudence would help us assess where to toss the bean bag and how hard to toss it.

To live virtuously, we must choose to act according to right reason—and there are many ways to miss the mark. To act virtuously, we must choose and perform the correct act, at the right time, in the right manner, in the right place, and for the right duration. This is incredibly challenging. In fact, it is impossible for us to achieve this consistently apart from grace (see chapter six). For this reason, we do not want to become scrupulous; to achieve virtue, it is enough for us to attain most of these circumstances, or at least not to miss any of them in a serious way. Since none of us is God, there will always be room for us to improve, but that does not mean that we cannot possess virtue at all.

Remember the difference between an intellectual virtue and a moral virtue? An intellectual virtue is a perfection of our reason, but it does not necessarily lead to good action, and so it is not a virtue in the fullest sense. It does not necessarily make the person good. A moral virtue, on the other hand, involves right action and does make the person good.

Prudence is unique among the virtues insofar as it is both an intellectual and a moral virtue. It does not merely stop at knowledge of what should be done in given circumstances (this could be simply the intellectual virtue of knowledge, such as knowledge of ethics), but prudence also inspires us to act on this knowledge. If prudence were to remain abstract knowledge, it would not make us good. However, since it goes beyond mere knowledge and moves us to act on that right knowledge, it is a virtue that makes us good.

For this reason, St. Thomas Aquinas calls prudence the "form of the virtues." What he means by this is that prudence, since it determines what is just, what is courageous, and what is temperate, gives shape to the other virtues.

Consider the analogy of a construction project. There are blueprints for how the building should be constructed, builders, and a foreman who reads the blueprints and directs the builders. In this analogy, prudence plays the role of both the blueprints (knowledge of what to do) and the foreman (inspiration to do the action), while the other moral virtues play the role of the builders (the virtues that help us to act well).

Lack of Prudence

Since prudence involves not only knowledge of how to act well but also the inspiration to do so, there are multiple ways in which someone can lack prudence. Without prudence, one cannot hit the target. Understanding how prudence can go wrong will help us to see why we are missing and to adjust accordingly. Imprudence is the name of the vice that is opposed to prudence by deficiency, but it can come in a variety of types.

Rashness is the vice of rushing into action without thinking about how we should act, such as the person who does not follow the wisdom of "look before you leap." Thoughtlessness is the vice of not considering whether our choices help us to reach a good goal. For example, a husband would be thoughtless if he desired to make his wife happy by surprising her with a gift he made (which is a good goal) but did not consider that in the process of making the gift he neglected to do the other things that his wife asked him to do (which will make her unhappy and therefore miss the good goal). Negligence is the vice of not paying attention to the relevant details and circumstances of a situation so that the person can make a truly prudent decision of how to act, since these circumstances are relevant for determining the virtuous mean.

While those three vices are all somehow deficient in reason, the vice of inconstancy is deficient in the second part of prudence: inspiring the person to act on her knowledge. The inconstant person does accurately determine what the virtuous action is, but when it comes time to perform the action, she does something else instead. Whether her motivation is laziness, fear, or something else, she misses the mark of prudence. A person who makes a correct list of priorities but then procrastinates and achieves none of them acts inconstantly, for example.

As an excess on the part of reasoning, scrupulosity is the vice of constantly deliberating about what to do to the point of never acting. This is the person who considers so many details and circumstances that she can never decide what she should do. It is an excessive investigation of the circumstances that lacks the ability to figure out which are important, which ultimately paralyzes the individual and prevents her from acting at all. How many times have we missed opportunities to do good because we overthought the situation! I remember a time when I kept going back and forth on whether I should attend a discernment retreat (the irony!). I had made a list of pros and cons, but I always found a way to make the list even, and so I could never decide. It took me so long to decide that the due date came and went, and I was not able to make my choice; instead, it was made for me.

On the part of action, craftiness is a vice that often looks like prudence because it achieves a good goal, but the crafty person does so by cutting corners, cheating, or defrauding others. In Luke 16:1–13, Jesus tells the parable of an unjust steward. A steward is entrusted to manage another's possessions. This steward was likely given the position because he seemed to be good with money, which may be a sign of prudence. However, as the story reveals, the steward made his money by defrauding and overcharging others, showing that he was not prudent but instead crafty: he achieved a good goal (wealth) by immoral means (fraud).

Justice and Injustice

Prudence is essential for being able to hit the targets of what is just, what is courageous, and what is temperate. However, without understanding what each of these other virtues are, we will not be able to be prudent (more on this in chapter four). Thus, if we are going to employ this chapter's strategy well—of identifying our vices and "overshooting" the virtuous target so that we hit it—we need to be aware of what our targets are. For this reason, we will look more closely here at justice, fortitude, and temperance.

Of all the cardinal virtues, justice may be the one that gets the most attention. This is likely because it is the virtue of maintaining right relationships with other people, and so it most directly affects others. Since it usually deals with external actions, it is also the easiest to observe. Technically speaking, justice is the habit of giving what we owe to another; injustice, then, is the vice of not giving what we owe to another. The vices opposed to justice are unique in that we do not have separate names for them; they are simply injustice by deficiency and injustice by excess.

Since justice is the virtue of treating others well, we can be unjust by either not giving what is due to our neighbor (injustice by deficiency) or unjust by demanding too much from our neighbor (injustice by excess). It is not fair, for example, to pay back my neighbor less than what I owe him. Nor is it fair to demand that he give me more than we agreed to. However, it could be generous, rather than unjust, to give to him more than what I owe him or to permit him to give me less than what he owes me.

But even generosity, itself a virtue, is a mean between extremes. One could be deficiently generous and possess the vice of stinginess or could give in excess of what is reasonable and acquire the vice of wastefulness. Once again, prudence determines what is reasonably generous in the given situation.

Justice has many other sub-virtues, generally categorized by different types of relationships. While we do not always have words in English to name the vices opposed to these virtues, there will always be at least one vice in excess of what is reasonable and one vice that does not meet what is reasonable. Some of our relationships are unequal. For example, God is an infinite being, worthy of all honor and worship. We, on the other hand, cannot and should not expect God to pay us honor and worship. So, one sub-virtue of justice, called *religion*, deals with giving God the right worship and understanding our proper place in relation to him. If we give God less than what is due to him, then we act from the vice of sloth. If we give worship to anything other than God—whether it be ourselves, a celebrity, money, or something else—we have the vice of idolatry.

Another unequal relationship is our relationship with our parents. Our parents gave us life and brought us into this world, and there is nothing we can do to repay them for that. Thus, we owe them acts of *piety* (the virtue of properly honoring one's parents or homeland). Along with piety we owe *obedience*, which in fact is due to any of our superiors. If we are deficiently obedient, we possess a vice of disobedience. If we are excessively obedient, we have a vice of slavishness.

While we are automatically in relationship with God and our parents, other relationships are freely and voluntary established. In other words, they are not necessary, but once we form them we find that they come with their own duties. For example, no one is obligated to become friends with anyone, but once you are someone's friend you now have certain expectations to fulfill for him (such as helping him when possible). Along with *friendship* and the above-mentioned *generosity*, the virtue of *kindness* falls into this category.

Finally, there are other sub-virtues that are due to all people, no matter what the type of relationship, such as *gratitude* and *honesty*. Even these virtues have their opposites (ingratitude and flattery opposed to gratitude, and dishonesty and bluntness or having "loose lips" opposed to honesty).

Temperance and Fortitude

The final two cardinal virtues can be treated together because they have a similar purpose—moderating our emotions so that they are reasonable. For sure, hitting the target of right emotions may be the hardest target of all! It may sound strange to think of our emotions as having any moral component, or to claim that they can be reasonable, because so often they seem out of our control. The reality is that the reason why our emotions so often are unreasonable and seemingly out of our control is because we are wounded by original sin. Sacred Scripture and Tradition both teach that before the Fall, human emotions were always reasonable, meaning that Adam and Eve would have felt the right emotions at the right time, toward the right things, and to the right degree.

We are not as fortunate, and although the sacrament of Baptism cleanses us from original sin, its effects remain. We often experience our emotions as mysterious or even foreign to us, claiming "That was not really me!" as they drag us away from doing what we know is right. There is perhaps nothing that captures this experience more clearly than the words of St. Paul: "I do not understand my own actions. For I do not do what I want, but I do the very thing I hate" (Romans 7:15).

The good news is that we have not lost all control over our emotions from original sin; they can be fully restored to right reason through the grace of Christ. The next chapter will explain four stages of growth toward virtue, and the final stage involves getting our desires right. Since understanding the emotions is more important for that strategy than the present one, we will come back to the emotions in more depth in the next chapter. For now, it is enough to note that all our emotions are morally neutral in themselves and only become good or evil based on the circumstances. Some of our emotions sound like they should always be good (for example, love, hope, and joy), but it would be bad, for example, to love sin, enjoy harming others, or hope that I can breathe underwater. Likewise, some emotions sound like they should always be bad (for example, hatred, sorrow, or fear), but it would be good to hate injustice, feel sorry for the pain I have caused others, or fear offending God and choosing hell.

While there is a wide range of emotions that we can experience, they can broadly be divided into simple emotions (those which we commonly experience throughout each day) and difficult emotions (those which we only experience when we encounter some obstacle or danger). Temperance is the virtue that ensures that our simple emotions are reasonable and that evil desires do not lead us into sin, while courage is the virtue that ensures that our difficult emotions are reasonable and that we do not allow obstacles and difficulties to deter us from doing what is right. Temperance is opposed by the very rare deficiency of insensibility, which takes no pleasure in things like food, drink, sex, or recreation, and by the excess of intemperance and all of its varieties (gluttony, drunkenness, lust, and luxuriousness). Fortitude (or courage) is opposed by the deficiency of cowardice and the excess of foolhardiness. Chapters four and five will provide many more illustrations of these virtues and vices we have covered. For now, it is time to use the knowledge of these habits that we already must live out using this chapter's strategy.

Hitting the Target by Overshooting It

Having established that virtue is a mean between two extremes and given many examples of virtues and their extremes, it is now possible to return to our cornhole analogy and see how this can help in the pursuit of virtue. It is also worth reflecting, at this point, on the virtues and vices that have been named. Which virtues do I see in myself? Which vices do I see in myself? Which vices did I not think were vices at all?

This last question is key. Aristotle notes a fundamental human observation: In general, all of us think that we are right and others are wrong. Thus, he teaches that those who possess a vice tend to view their vice as itself a virtuous mean between two extremes, and to think that what is a virtue is actually a vice!

For example, when I was younger, I was terrified of confrontation and avoided it as much as possible. I viewed all confrontation as mean and vicious. Over time, I came to see that confronting another person is sometimes the most loving and courageous thing to do (as Jesus says in Matthew 18), and that I possessed the vice of cowardice, not a virtue of gentleness. In a similar vein, most people who are lustful see chastity as prudishness, most narcissistic people see humility as slavishness, and most imprudent people see prudence as foolishness. To return to the story of the snake, a cowardly person would have viewed my action as foolhardy, believing that the courageous thing would be to run away. He would take this view because he would overestimate the danger of the situation. Likewise, a foolhardy person would view my action as cowardly since I was not willing to pick up the snake with my hands.

This observation factors into our current strategy. If I need to grow in a particular virtue, it is likely that I possess a contrary vice. It is also likely, therefore, that I perceive the virtue as itself a vice. This means that, until I can accurately perceive the virtue for its reasonableness, I must bring myself to act in a way that seems extreme in order to do what is actually reasonable. I must seemingly overshoot the target in order to actually hit it.

In cornhole, I had a habit of undershooting the board and had to toss the bean bag in a way that I thought was too forceful in order to land on the board.

Similarly, in the pursuit of virtue, I may need to perform an act that seems to overshoot the virtue in order to actually attain it. The cowardly person sees courage as foolhardiness, so he has to do something he thinks is foolhardy in order to be courageous; the lustful person sees chastity as prudish, and so he must act in a way that he thinks is prudish to be chaste. In time, as these truly virtuous activities become habits for us, we will come to see that the courage was not foolhardiness but in fact courage, and the chastity was not prudishness but in fact chastity. The more we act reasonably, the more our very reasoning is purified and allows us to see situations and our actions for what they truly are.

When Aristotle describes this strategy, he uses the analogy of straightening bent wood. If the wood is bent in one direction, you must bend it in the opposite direction to make it straight. Just so, if we bend toward one vice, we must bend toward the opposite vice to become straight. For example, a person who has the vice of gluttony by eating too much must eat less to become temperate. We do not want the gluttonous person to become unhealthy and eat too little. However, this is not likely to happen. The gluttonous person is used to eating a lot of food, so any amount less than what he normally eats will seem to be "too little"; any smaller amount of food, in his eyes, will be overly abstemious. However, his perception is off. The smaller amount of food is, in fact, temperate. From his perspective, his normal eating habit is virtuous, and anything less is vicious. So once he recognizes that his habit is not virtuous, he must aim for what seems to him to be the opposite vice, but is in reality the virtue.

The idea is that, since we already view the virtue as an extreme, we are not very likely to overshoot the virtue so much that we actually end up acquiring the opposite vice. It is not likely that a gluttonous person will actually end up emaciated or that a lustful person will actually become prudish, or that a cowardly person will actually become foolhardy. The very fact that we already view the virtue as extreme is self-limiting for us in that regard. For this reason, this strategy is not counseling people to develop extreme or unhealthy behavior. Rather, a person with a vice is already unhealthy insofar as he misapprehends what is reasonable behavior. The strategy is meant to correct this misapprehension. As the person practices this new pattern of behavior, the right action will help him to perceive it as it truly is and eventually see it as virtuous. As with cornhole, it may feel weird at first to toss the bean bag harder, but once you start hitting the board, that amount of force feels right. Likewise, it may feel weird for the gluttonous person to eat less, but after a while he recognizes that it is not actually too little food but instead the reasonable amount.

St. Thomas Aquinas, commenting on Aristotle, states that this strategy for growing in virtue is most effective, but it is not the easiest. It is theoretically possible that some people may swing like a pendulum from one extreme to the other. If you are an impulsive person, this may be something to look out for. Having a trusted accountability partner (see chapter five) who can point out when our swings are too wild is helpful. Even if one does swing from one extreme to the other, and back again, as long as she is concertedly striving for virtue, these swings should get less and less extreme until she settles at the virtuous midpoint. It may take some time for our prudence to calibrate correctly, but if we persevere and continue to reflect on our choices, we will locate the true target.

Again, swinging to the opposite vice usually does not occur because one's misperception of the virtuous mean already limits how far that "overshot" will be. Rather than swing to the opposite extreme, it is more likely that the individual will simply fail at his attempt to shoot for the opposite extreme—because it feels so unnatural to his habits—and will make no progress.

While this strategy is advocated by both thinkers,[5] it must be understood correctly in order to truly lead to virtue. Due to this potential for misunderstandings, some may opt for an alternative strategy, which the next chapter will discuss. Aristotle and Aquinas both also counsel a more gradual strategy for growing in virtue that people who do not have success with the current strategy may find more effective. It is to this gradual strategy that we now turn.

Strategies

1. Fake it till you make it.

 2. Overshoot the target – Vice can obscure our perception of what is virtuous so we must aim beyond what we feel is virtuous in order to attain virtue.

3

Breaking the Habit

In the first chapter we observed how the path to virtue requires more than mere repetition of acts and that only increasing the intensity of our good habits will cause them to grow. Chapter two explained one strategy for increasing this intensity: aiming for the opposite extreme and drastically altering our behavior. While both Aristotle and St. Thomas Aquinas agree that this can be an effective strategy for cultivating virtue, they also admit that it is difficult, and this difficulty prevents some from trying it. While no strategy for growing in virtue will be easy, there are some strategies that may be less difficult.

This chapter will focus on an alternate strategy that Aristotle and St. Thomas present—namely, slowly withdrawing from our vices. Whereas the previous strategy involved immediately trying to achieve the virtuous mean by radically altering our behavior, this present strategy involves focusing on our smaller acts and incrementally moving closer to the virtuous mean. While it may take longer than the previous strategy, its gradual approach may be easier to swallow for many.

It is easy to get discouraged. I cannot count the number of times that I have decided to start an exercise routine by planning out a whole series of exercises, only to quit after a few days. When faced with a radical change from not exercising to spending a half hour per day exercising, it is all too easy to find excuses to skip a day. Instead, I have had the most success with maintaining exercise routines when I start off very small but then make sure that I do it every day, and only slowly increase the number of repetitions and length of exercise.

We can experience similar discouragement in the moral life. I remember a time when I decided that I wanted to grow in selflessness. I made big plans regarding how I would make sandwiches and deliver them to the homeless, and how I would volunteer at different charitable organizations. In the end, I did none of it. The task was too daunting. And so I made no progress in selflessness. But, since then, I have realized I can try to focus instead on the little ways that I can be selfless each day: small sacrifices of my time helping others when I would rather do something else; looking for ways that I can help my wife or children; making myself available to coworkers rather than rushing to my office and closing the door before anyone can see me. None of these acts is anything deserving of a statue in my honor in the city square, but I am confident that this strategy is heading me in the right direction.

Here and Now

This is the advantage of this chapter's strategy: *breaking the habit*. It avoids the risk that we may feel too daunted by our grandiose plans, and instead it focuses realistically on what we can do here and now, in this very moment. If we only make plans, those plans may always remain in the future. If we focus on the present moment, there is always some way that we can practice virtue.

What is God calling me to do right now? To focus on this project rather than to procrastinate? To give this person my time rather than to rush away? To pass on dessert rather than to indulge? Focusing on the present moment turns the great mountain of moral perfection into a molehill of one good act. And rather than despairing over a failed grand endeavor, one can continue to be motivated through many small successes.

We should recognize that this strategy comes with its own set of temptations that we must avoid, most notably the temptation to become complacent. Once we have made some measurable progress, it is easy to decide that is enough for now. It's easy to say, "I'll try to grow in more virtue ... later." But that "later" may never come. This strategy will require great perseverance and can be assisted by an accountability partner (more on that in chapter five). But the more we persevere in it, the more successes we will have and the more we should be encouraged to strive for greater and greater excellence.

This chapter will look at the stages of growth from a vice to a virtue, identifying the relevant markers of each stage so that we can not only identify where we stand in relation to virtue but also identify the specific aspects that we need to focus on in order to continue to withdraw from vice and make moral progress.

We Are Souls and Bodies

When thinking of how we can overcome our vices, we sometimes jump to grandiose ideas and set large goals that are too great to achieve. It has become a sort of running joke in our culture how everyone makes sweeping New Year's resolutions but will have abandoned them all before the end of January. But how often do we set a resolution for the month, or for the week, or even for the day or hour? These goals would be much easier to achieve and can give us the necessary motivation to see the year-long resolutions through to their end.

Catholics also tend to over-spiritualize these vices, taking them to the sacrament of Reconciliation time and again and then wondering why we are not improving. I vividly remember learning this lesson one time at confession. I confessed to the priest, among other sins, the anger I had been feeling, usually about very small matters, and how I knew that I should be more grateful and patient but instead was letting everything get to me. I wanted to eliminate this moral imperfection (even if not necessarily a sin) in me and thought the only way I could do so was through God's grace. The priest's response caught me off guard: "How much sleep have you been getting?" "Um ... uh ... Not as much as I should be, Father." He replied, "Make sure you get more sleep, then." Sure enough, I started going to bed earlier and I found that, suddenly, I was much more patient and in a better mood.

We have a tendency to forget that we are not just souls who make use of a body, but that we are in fact embodied souls; we are our souls, and we are our bodies. This is why we believe in the resurrection of everyone's bodies at the end of time; without our bodies, we are not fully human! The soul is simply what gives life to the body, and what we do in the body is an expression of our soul. It is no wonder, then, that just as our souls can influence our bodies (think of how physically weighed down or even sick you can feel when you have not been to confession for a while or know that you have hurt someone), so also our bodies can have an effect on our souls. Lack of sleep leads to lack of patience and kindness—who knew?

This is where we can return to those New Year's resolutions. If we make a resolution to "overcome anger" or to "lose twenty pounds" in the coming year, the surest way to achieve these goals is to set smaller goals along the way, and many of them can be as easy as just taking care of our bodies. While we should always resort to prayer for God's assistance, there are some basic and simple things we can do to get the ball rolling—although they are not always easy for us to do! In the next chapter we will even see how these small acts can sometimes surprisingly help us to grow in virtues that seem unrelated.

Natural Dispositions

On the topic of our bodies, we are all born with different bodily dispositions. The human body can possess a wide range of different sizes, colors, health conditions, and anomalies. Since we are embodied souls, the makeup of our bodies often influences our habits of activity. For example, smaller people are often naturally more timid, while taller people are often naturally more confident. This is not always the case—we do have the ability to act contrary to these bodily influences—but it is a relevant factor when we look at the natural dispositions of the soul.

In chapter one, we discussed dispositions, which differ from habits because they are caused by any act and are easily changed. Over time, they may strengthen into a true habit. While it is possible to acquire a disposition through any of our actions, it is also true that we enter life with certain natural dispositions of our soul. Some of these are influenced by our bodily makeup, while others are simply present for reasons that we do not understand. Some people are naturally patient; others are naturally complainers. Some people are naturally kind and giving; others are naturally mean and selfish. Some people are naturally quiet; others are naturally social. It can take some digging and reflection to unearth our natural dispositions, although they do tend to come to the surface in times of great anxiety. In these situations, we may default to our natural temperament.

As a parent, I am mindful of my children's natural dispositions. Both are well-behaved, but they definitely have their own personalities. I remember when one of them was just a toddler. He loved blueberries and had been snacking on them. He finished the bowl and asked for more, but my wife told him that he was done (she did not want a blue diaper!). He asked again, "Please more blueberries?" "No." "Please more blueberries?" "No." "Please..." "No!" He paused for a few seconds, then asked, "Mama, can I have milk?" "Why, certainly!" And then, as my wife opened the refrigerator door, my son zipped under her arm and grabbed the blueberries. I was not sure whether to laugh and be proud that my son could devise such as scheme or be concerned that he was already doing so at such a young age. Whatever emotion I should have been feeling, one thing was certain: my son had a natural disposition toward craftiness rather than prudence, and I would have to help him with that in the future.

While it may be easier to see these tendencies in our children than in ourselves, it is important to reflect on our own dispositions so that we can work against our vices. The first step in withdrawing from vices is to identify our natural dispositions of soul. What type of behavior are we naturally inclined toward? What patterns do we see in our choices and activities? It is important to identify these because they are the dispositions that we came into the world with. They are the easiest ways for us to act and, even if we have overcome some of them and changed our behavior, they are the sorts of behavior that we are likely to retreat into in periods of stress and difficulty.

Knowing ourselves and knowing both our natural strengths and weaknesses of character will make us aware of not only what temptations we will likely face, but also which good qualities can help us to avoid them. For example, if I am naturally disposed to cowardice but also naturally disposed to justice, then I may be able to use my sense of justice to help overcome my fears (more on this in chapter four). Self-knowledge helps us to live out this chapter's strategy of step by step withdrawing from vice because, by identifying our vices, temptations, and general weaknesses, we can assess what patterns of behavior, environmental factors, or states of mind are contributing to them. Once we identify what contributes to them, we can establish a plan for how we will remove them from our lives, thereby opening a clear path to obtaining virtue.

Custom

While nature has a large influence on our fundamental behaviors, nurture also plays a significant role. We have seen how custom acts as a pseudo-habit. While it does not engage reason and free choice to the extent that a true virtue or vice does, it does create consistent patterns of behavior that we may be hesitant to change. We might form a customary pattern of behavior by unthinkingly following our natural dispositions for years. Or a pattern might arise out of the way we were raised or social trends. As with natural dispositions, our customs could be conducive to either virtues or vices.

While our natural dispositions can be difficult to change because they are comfortable to us, custom can be difficult to change because of social pressure, especially if others interpret our change as a judgment on their behavior or a rejection of them personally. However, if the custom is truly preventing us from virtue, we cannot allow this pressure to deter our pursuit.

While natural dispositions and customs are significant influences on the habits of character that we develop, none of them ever reaches the status of a full-fledged habit: a stable and habitual disposition of character that arises from deliberation and free choice. With some focused effort, both natural disposition and custom can be overcome and changed. Eventually, though, our natural dispositions, custom, and free choices settle into virtues or vices. Our virtues and vices become deeply engrained within us, to the point of becoming a second nature, such that anyone who knows us well would be able to predict our behavior in different situations with high probability.

Vice to Virtue

Since our goal is to grow in virtue, we will focus on the stages of growth from a vice to a virtue, noting relevant features of each stage, so we can clearly see where we can make small steps toward virtue. We can use this four-stage schema either to look at our entire moral character (for example, am I overall a virtuous or vicious person?) or to look at whether we possess an individual virtue (for example, am I impatient or patient?). This schema will help us to pinpoint exactly what part of our bad habits we must break, and what specifically to focus on as we withdraw step by step from vice.

These four stages of growth, again, come from the thought of Aristotle and St. Thomas Aquinas. From worst to best, they include *vice, incontinence, continence,* and *virtue.* While we have mentioned virtue and vice throughout the book, this is the first time we have mentioned continence and incontinence. Ignore any associations your mind may make between these terms and the names of aisles at your local pharmacy. Both terms derive from the word for "contain," which in this context refers to our ability (or inability) to contain our emotions when they are unreasonable. The continent person succeeds in containing these irrational emotions, while the incontinent person is unable to contain them, thus allowing these unreasonable emotions to pull him away from choosing and acting on what is good.

Before delving more deeply into each stage and explaining strategies for growth from one to the next, it will be helpful to get a big-picture view of all four of them. Since virtue is the fullness of moral perfection, every other stage is going to lack some aspect of this perfection. So, to understand these stages, it is simplest to consider what elements are necessary for a virtue and then show what the other stages lack.

Up to this point, we have made frequent reference to human reason, free will, and emotions. In theology, these constitute different "powers" or "capacities" of the soul. As the principle of life within us, our soul has a variety of capacities. Some of them, such as the capacities to grow, reproduce, see, taste, and use the other senses, we only have indirect control over at best. For example, we can take medicine to help with indigestion, but we cannot will ourselves to grow another inch; we can wear glasses to see better, but we cannot will ourselves to have 20/20 vision. As such, we do not call someone immoral for wearing glasses or immoral for being short. It is something out of our control.

We do, however, have direct control over what we think, what we will and choose, and, to some extent, how we feel. Thus, the intellect, will, and emotions are three capacities of the soul that we do recognize as having moral weight. We call someone immoral who thinks that theft is good, or who takes pleasure in the suffering of others, while we call someone moral who chooses to serve the poor. So, if virtue is the fullness of moral perfection, then it is going to entail the right use of all these capacities. There will be a harmony between the individual's intellect, will, and emotions, such that they are all on the same page and work in union for the good. This is true human excellence.

Habituating the Emotions

But how exactly do our emotions have a moral component? I do not imagine that anyone in their right mind would deny that between two people, one who helps a neighbor willingly and with great joy, and another who helps a neighbor begrudgingly and with constant complaining, all other things being equal, that there is no greater excellence displayed in the joyful person than in the miserable one. If virtue is a perfection of our character, and it is more perfect to be joyful in helping than to be grumpy in helping, then emotions have something to contribute to virtue. Without reasonable emotions, we have not yet reached perfection of character.

To take another example, we can see that it is wrong for a police officer to have great enjoyment in finding any way he can to write someone a ticket and to catch a driver on as many charges as possible as opposed to an officer who will write tickets only if necessary and is more concerned with correcting the violators so that there will be a greater level of safety in the community. The first officer takes delight in the suffering of others, while the second experiences sorrow in the illegal activity of others while seeking to correct that behavior for the good of the violator and of society. While both officers perform the same action in writing a ticket, the first officer's intention is to do harm, while the second's is to do good. Each are driven by their emotions. Thus, our emotions can help us to do the right thing for the right reason, or the right thing for the wrong reason. Clearly, the one with reasonable emotions is more perfect.

Therefore, our emotions, like our actions, can contribute to or impede our true human excellence, and thereby have a moral weight. Yet there are two important things to remember when evaluating the morality of emotions. First, while we can cultivate our emotions to become more reasonable, on this side of heaven there may always be some occasions where we are caught off guard and emotively respond in an involuntary way. No matter how much a person works at restraining fear, for example, there is always a chance he can be surprised from behind and let out a scream.

Second, we must keep in mind that our emotions are morally neutral in themselves, and that any expressed emotion can be good or evil, depending on the circumstances. This can be confusing because we have negative associations with some emotions (sorrow, anger, fear, aversion, despair) and positive associations with others (love, desire, pleasure, hope). To take the examples given above, notice that it was good for the person to take joy in helping his neighbor, but it was bad for the officer to take joy in writing tickets for its own sake. Likewise, it was bad for the person to be averse to helping his neighbor, but it may be good for an officer to be averse to giving too many tickets, or at least to have some restraint. Further, it could be good to hope to do well on a test, but foolish to hope to be able to fly. It is good to have a healthy fear of death, but bad to have a serious fear of mushrooms hidden in your meal. Any emotion can be morally good or bad depending on what we feel the emotion toward and the given circumstances.

Unsurprisingly, it is prudence that determines what emotions are reasonably called for in given circumstances, and it is prudence that can help to make our emotions more reasonable. To take up again the example of being afraid of clowns: since it is irrational to be afraid of clowns, one can conquer the fear by thinking more reasonably about the situation. This may take certain steps such as speaking with off-duty clowns, seeing them without their costumes, and the like, but if one is able to see the situation truthfully—that a clown is just a regular person dressed up to entertain people—one can slowly train his emotions to become more reasonable and cease to fear clowns ... although a healthy aversion to them may remain.

Simple and Difficult Emotions

As we saw in the last chapter, prudence and temperance, two of the cardinal virtues, regulate our emotions so they are reasonable. The reason why there are two cardinal virtues that moderate our emotions is that, traditionally, philosophers and theologians alike have counted eleven basic emotions that fall into two categories. The first six emotions are called simple emotions. As we mentioned in the last chapter, these are emotions we commonly experience throughout the day. They have to do with whether we are positively or negatively inclined toward something we experience. If we are inclined toward it, we experience *love*. If it is not present to us, we experience *desire*; if it is present to us, we experience *joy* or pleasure. If we are not inclined toward something, we experience *hatred* for it. If it is not present to us, we experience *aversion* or disgust; if it is present to us, we experience *sorrow* or misery.

The Simple Emotions

Emotion we experience toward something that we are positively inclined toward:⟶ Initial inclination: *Love*

| When the thing is not present: *Desire* | When the thing is present: *Joy* |

Emotion we experience toward something that we are negatively inclined toward:⟶ Initial inclination: *Hatred*

| When the thing is not present: *Aversion* | When the thing is present: *Sorrow* |

These are the simple emotions, and we experience them all of the time toward everything that we sense, whether we realize it or not. While they do allow for some breadth of subjectivity (some people may enjoy sweet foods while others enjoy savory foods), there is also objectivity (for example, we should all hate sin and love virtue).

To repeat, we experience these simple emotions toward everything that we sense. Sometimes these emotions are strong and noticeable, such as feeling butterflies in our chest when our loved one comes by, or feeling sorrow and crying when a love one has passed. Most of the time, we do not even notice these emotions because they are so slight. At this very moment, you have an emotive response to the place where you are sitting—probably one of pleasure, or else you would get up and move to a more comfortable spot. You also are having an emotive response to the very words you are reading—hopefully one of great pleasure and excited desire to read on.

A second set of emotions is only experienced in the midst of some difficulty or danger, and these are the five difficult emotions mentioned in the previous chapter: we experience *hope* when some difficult good is within our grasp and achievable and *despair* when it eludes us; we experience *fear* when some difficult evil approaches us and *aggression* when we sense that it is receding; finally, we experience *anger* when a difficult or dangerous evil is present to us. Anger is the only emotion without a contrary because we experience joy or pleasure when a difficult good is finally achieved.

While we do not perceive all of the things we sense to be obstacles or dangers, there are certainly many obstacles that we encounter throughout the day that

----

The Difficult Emotions

Emotion toward something difficult/dangerous that is good:

When the thing is achievable: *Hope*	When the thing is out of reach: *Despair*

Emotion toward something difficult/dangerous that is evil:

When the thing approaches: *Fear*	When the thing is receding: *Aggression*

When the thing is present: *Anger*

----

give rise to these emotions. We might hope that our morning commute will be smooth, only to encounter road construction and begin to despair that we will ever get to work on time. We might fear having a difficult conversation with someone, while our emotion turns to aggression when we have practiced what we will say a few times.

Again, we must remember to put aside our usual associations with these terms and recognize that any emotion can be good or bad, reasonable or not, depending on the situation. These are the eleven emotions, and any other type of emotion (such as pity) arises from the combination of two or more emotions. This understanding of emotion can help us as we examine our reactions and work on building virtue step by step.

Visualizing the Stages of Moral Growth

Returning to the three capacities of our soul that we can control reasonably and are thereby moral (intellect, will, and emotions), we can derive four elements that are necessary for a truly virtuous act. First, the person must know what actions are good. However, when we looked at prudence in the previous chapter, we noted that it is not enough simply to know what is good, but we must also choose to act on it. Just as prudence determines what is good and inspires us to do it, so also the second element necessary for virtue is to choose the good action. Third, it is no good to choose a good action if it is never performed, so the person must also do the good action. Finally, the perfection of virtue rests not only in doing the good action, but also in enjoying it. This means we have four elements necessary for virtue: 1) knowing the good, 2) choosing the good, 3) doing the good, and 4) enjoying the good.

Four Stages of Moral Growth

	Right Knowledge	Right Choice	Right Act	Right Enjoyment
Virtue	✓	✓	✓	✓
Continence	✓	✓	✓	X
Incontinence	✓	✓	X	X
Vice	✓	X	X	X

From here we will see that each stage below virtue is lacking more and more of these four elements. The continent person knows the good, chooses the good, and performs the good, but can only do so by containing his unreasonable emotions that pull him away from the good. As a result, the continent person does not enjoy doing the good. The incontinent person knows the good and chooses it, so she has the first two elements of virtue. But since she is unable to contain her irrational emotions, these emotions pull her away from right reason and so she neither performs the good nor enjoys it. Finally, the vicious person has some understanding of the good, but does not choose it, perform it, or enjoy it. In fact, the vicious person chooses, performs, and enjoys evil acts.

Before looking more closely at each stage, it is worth reiterating that this schema can be applied to either a person in general or a particular habit of a person. For example, an individual may conclude, from these descriptions, that he is overall continent. However, at a specific level he may find himself to be continent in most virtues but incontinent in others, or continent in some habits but vicious in others. Let us now look at each stage individually, starting with vice, in order to discover strategies for taking small steps toward the highest stage—virtue.

Vice

The etymology of our word "vice" sheds light on its meaning. Vice derives from the Latin *vitium*, from which we also derive the word "vitiate." To vitiate something is to impair its quality, to corrupt it in some way. In the case of vice, what is corrupted is our very nature, drawing us to act in a way that is less human (that is, free and rational) and more like an animal (that is, irrational and a slave to base desires).

In the case of virtue, we find the intellect, will, and emotions all integrated for a single cause. Vice, on the other hand, dis-integrates our souls. It does this by first pitting our emotions against our reason, and then by drawing the will away from reason, and lastly by corrupting our reason itself.

It is no wonder that Scripture reveals to us that "the wages of sin is death" (Romans 6:23). If the soul, which gives life to our body, is unable to remain integrated among its own capacities, it makes sense that it will eventually be forced to depart from the body. This then results in the death of the body which literally disintegrates. The literal disintegration of our bodies is the sign of the dis-integrity of our souls due to sin. Fortunately, by the merits of Christ's passion and death, we will one day be reunited with our bodies, and if we have died to sin, we will experience the complete integration of the capacities within the soul, as well as the soul with the body, such that we will never die again.

As noted in the previous section, vice entails knowledge of what is good, but no choice, performance, or enjoyment of what is good. In fact, vice typically involves enjoyment of what is evil. But what does it mean to say that a vicious person has one element of virtue—knowledge of what is good? The nature of the knowledge of what is good is curious. The vicious person must have some understanding of what is good, otherwise he would be invincibly ignorant and therefore would not be culpable for his actions.

When it comes to ignorance of ethics, someone can either be *invincibly ignorant*—meaning, their ignorance could not be overcome through their own reasonable efforts—or *vincibly ignorant*—meaning, their ignorance could be overcome through their own efforts. For example, if a child was raised in a society of thieves, was taught how to steal from a young age, and never encountered the Gospel, that child may be invincibly ignorant to the fact that theft is immoral. Since the child's ignorance is no fault of his, he is not culpable. That is, he is not morally responsible for the actions he performs from that ignorance.

In my own case, I can only think of one time that I was invincibly ignorant of my wrongdoing. There was a stretch of road that I used to take on my commute, and it was one of those ambiguous types of road where you cannot intuit what the speed limit would be. It was not a residential area, but neither was it a true highway. It had some curves, but it was two lanes. The problem was that I could not locate a single speed limit sign on that stretch of road. I would search all along the road whenever I drove down it, but to no avail. I was terrified of getting pulled over but could only make my best guess at the speed limit based off of the type of road and the speed of the other cars. One day, I finally found the speed limit sign—it had been obscured by tree branches and vines. It was only because the road crew had come and cleared the overgrowth that the sign was visible again. And it was then that I found out that the speed limit was ten miles slower than I had guessed! I was relieved to finally know the limit, and even more relieved that I had never been pulled over. If I had been, hopefully the officer would have had mercy considering that I had no way of knowing the actual speed limit in those days before GPS.

Invincible ignorance is rare; most of our ignorance is vincible. For example, if a child was never explicitly taught that stealing is wrong but heard from a friend that it is, he has the means to ask reliable authorities whether stealing is, in fact, immoral. If he does not and simply assumes that stealing is morally acceptable, then he acts with vincible ignorance; he could have and should have known better. Likewise, in most cases where a person does not know the speed limit on a road, it is because he has not made enough effort to look for the speed limit sign, to remember it, or, nowadays, to turn on the GPS to tell him.

The moral evaluation of vincible ignorance can become quite complex, depending on why the person is ignorant and whether the person deliberately fostered that ignorance. Such ignorance could lessen one's moral responsibility (but not eliminate it) or increase one's responsibility and blameworthiness. We do not need to get bogged down in this analysis. It is enough for our purpose to note that the vicious person must have some knowledge of the good, otherwise no one would be blameworthy for vice. Whatever ignorance he has must be vincible and is likely self-imposed.

First Steps

This analysis of the knowledge of the vicious person sheds light on the necessary step that needs to be taken to start withdrawing from vice. What separates the vicious person from the incontinent person is that the incontinent person at least chooses to do the good, while the vicious person does not. That means that the incontinent person sees the goodness of sound moral choices, while the vicious person does not.

The vicious person has some understanding of morality, such as knowing what is against the law or what God commands, but he does not understand it fully; his priorities are disordered. While he may know that theft is evil, he thinks the good of acquiring wealth is more important. While he may know that Catholics are obliged to attend Mass every Sunday, he thinks enjoying golfing is more important.

Thus, the vicious person possesses only pseudo-knowledge, or partial knowledge, of the good. He pays some lip service to the truth of morality but does not truly understand it in his heart. The first step toward virtue, then, is to acquire this knowledge and to form one's conscience well.

This can be a difficult first step! For one, a vicious person may not have any desire to change, and so he would not seek to educate himself about morality. This is where the prayers of others come in; through prayer, God can inspire a desire for change in the individual so that he seeks conversion. Once the person does desire to seek virtue, the advice remains the same: pray! God, who is Truth itself, is best able to teach us right from wrong, but he will typically do this through others.

Beyond praying for truth (a strategy that will be explained more in chapter six), the next step is to simply be open to being taught morality. No one likes to be wrong or corrected, but all of us are ignorant about something. Often, the greatest obstacle in the way of our moral progress is our pride, thinking that we have it all figured out and know better than everyone else. If we are to withdraw from vice at all, we need to be open to being taught that our worldview may be upside down and that we need to change our habits.

Again, the strategy being laid out here is not one of radical change in behavior (as in chapter two), but one of gradual and calculated progress. We may learn that we have many vices, but short of a miracle we will not be able to overcome them all at once. Instead, pick one vice to work on and, even then, some small and achievable way to work on it.

The way out of vice is to start choosing good actions, so the best way to make this a habit is by doing it as often as possible, and the small opportunities will present themselves much more frequently than the big opportunities.

Setting Up for Success

Thus, the path out of vice is twofold: to come to a deeper understanding of what is good (and why it is good), and to practice choosing that good. Even if we are mostly unsuccessful in the beginning in following through with good actions, we can at least progress to incontinence if our intention is to do the good.

But we want to level the playing field as much as possible. Chances are, if we are mired in a vice, we likely have surrounded ourselves with things that promote that vice. So, to facilitate our efforts in choosing the good, we need to withdraw from those things that tempt us to sin.

If our vice is constant gossiping, we may have to withdraw from certain conversations or even certain friendships. If our vice is looking at pornography, we may need to withdraw from time spent alone or from time spent on the computer. If our vice is gluttony, we may need to withdraw from buying certain foods or eating out at restaurants. In my life, I recognized that certain music was contributing to me having bad moods and immoral thoughts. It was at first painful and sorrowful for me to stop listening to that music, but I believed the goal of becoming more cheerful was more important than listening to any music, and so it was a worthy sacrifice.

It is possible that our virtues will one day become strong enough that we can reclaim some of these things, but, until then, there is no reason to believe that our choices will change if our environment does not. To make the choice for the good easier, we have to remove those influences that tempt us to remain in our vice.

Incontinence

Once someone develops habits of understanding what is good and choosing it, they have reached the stage of incontinence. They have left vice behind and now have two of the elements of virtue instead of just one. But they still have work to do. Incontinent people reason well about what should be done, but they still have great difficulty in performing it.

The incontinent person is the one who is unable to contain his irrational emotions. If this pattern is habitual, it means that the person consistently chooses the wrong acts because her irrational emotions are so strong that they drag her away from what she knows she should do. Everyone experiences moments of incontinence (even the virtuous person, as we saw with St. Paul), but these occasions should become less and less frequent as we develop our virtues.

For better or for worse, a person is not able to remain in the state of incontinence for very long. If he did, he would probably have a nervous breakdown, because he would always be doing the very things he did not want to do. More likely, the incontinent person will either give up and return to vice or otherwise develop the strength of will to resist his irrational passions and become continent.

The focus for someone advancing from incontinence to continence will again be coming to a deeper understanding of why certain actions are good. Why is this? Because the mean of a virtue is a rational mean, and therefore it is a deeper grasp of the reasonableness of an activity that lends strength to our habits. While the incontinent person does understand what actions are good, the fact that he consistently gives into irrational emotions that cause him to perform evil acts shows that, in the moment, he views those evil acts as better for him than the good acts.

Thus, the incontinent person needs to spend more time reflecting on his choices to truly internalize why certain acts are better than others, even if in the moment they seem to lead to less pleasure. In essence, this is a stage of moral immaturity, where the person needs to learn the value of delayed gratification, just as we teach young children.

For example, a person with an alcohol problem needs to internalize the truth that, while it may feel enjoyable for the night to drink excessively, he will feel much better in the long run if he drinks moderately or abstains altogether. He will not suffer headaches, nausea, embarrassment, or the fallout of other bad decisions. Similarly, someone with a habit of staying up too late at night and missing sleep needs to reflect on her actions. Perhaps there is always something else she would rather be doing, whether it is hanging out with friends, watching a movie, or surfing the Internet. She has to really convince herself that getting more sleep would be better for her than staying up to enjoy those other activities.

The other important strategy for the incontinent person is to find ways to ensure that she follows through with her choices. This is because the main difference between the continent and the incontinent person is that the continent person actually performs the good act. To learn to follow through, the incontinent person might express her choices (such as to avoid drunkenness, avoid gossiping, get to bed on time, or the like) to a reliable friend in order to hold herself accountable or to be physically aided by the friend (more on this in chapter five). Or perhaps she will set small goals for herself and reward herself when she has had a certain number of successes. The key at this stage is to make sure that we are following through with our choices, and in time those choices will become easier as our will becomes stronger and better able to resist our irrational emotions.

Continence

Continence is a great achievement in the moral life, and while it may not have the perfection of virtue, it is certainly praiseworthy. Everyone loves the story of someone who overcame great obstacles to achieve something good, and in this case the great obstacle is our own irrational desires. The continent person is the one whose will is strong enough to contain unreasonable emotions such that they do not cause her to choose against her better judgment and right reason. She performs the good act despite these contrary emotions.

There are countless examples of continent acts—the person who forgives another when she would rather remain upset; the person who turns down another beer when all he can think of is how good it would taste; the person who helps his neighbor build a shed when all he wants is to stay home and watch the big game. In all these cases, the person's emotions and desires are driving them away from the good action, but the person nevertheless chooses the good action in spite of them.

For many people, apart from grace, continence may be the destination. This is not because people are incapable of acting virtuously, but because it is very difficult to bring our emotions into harmony with right reason. So what is our strategy here?

To truly enjoy the good activity—to the point where we do not desire something contrary—we really need to deeply internalize the goodness of the act and to understand, in our heart of hearts, its goodness. We understand that the goodness of this act derives from the very goodness of God, and the performance of it is a perfection of our human nature and the image of God within us. We desire to perform the activity simply because it is good, and not only for some external motivator. In order to achieve this, one either needs a deep conversion experience or a lot of time spent reflecting on the goodness of virtuous acts.

It is also possible, however, that simply the experience of doing good works can itself open our eyes to the beauty of the good. Simply the practice of good works can awaken in us an enjoyment of and desire for them. Sometimes we approach good works with a preconceived idea that we will not enjoy them, only to find that we do. As time goes on, we may find that these acts are more enjoyable than what we usually spend our time on.

Virtue

For those able to habituate their emotions to become reasonable, they will progress from the stage of continence to virtue. The virtuous person understands deeply the goodness of good activity, chooses these activities, and performs them with great enjoyment, or at least not with misery. (St. Thomas is a realist: He admits that for certain actions—such as being martyred—it is sufficient for virtue simply not to be sad. We would not expect someone to sing for joy while being eaten by lions.) For this reason, the hallmarks of the virtuous person are to act with ease, promptness, and enjoyment.

We can say the virtuous person acts with ease, because he does not suffer any internal tug-of-war between his reason and emotions. He acts with promptness, because he has already thought deeply about good actions and can intuit in any situation how best to act. Finally, he acts with enjoyment, because he would not rather be doing anything else.

It may seem strange to think about enjoying some of the good works that we do for ourselves and others, but wouldn't life be so much better if we did? Who would not want to experience the joy of being fully integrated, of not being at war with oneself and seeing oneself as his own worst enemy? Who would not want to approach all things reasonably and never have regrets?

We can think of St. Thérèse of Lisieux, who with childlike simplicity viewed every person and situation as a gift from God and desired nothing more than to be used by God for the conversion of others. We can think of St. Damien, who had such a love for every human that he would not let the risk of contracting leprosy keep him from tending to the marginalized. We can think of Jesus himself, who lived such a short life on earth but one that was full of true friendships (think of how he wept at the death of Lazarus), obedience to his parents, courage in his mission, and unconditional love for his enemies. If vice makes us utterly predictable, Jesus is the perfect example of how the life of virtue is dynamic, spontaneous, and liberating. None of his disciples or his enemies seemed able to predict what Jesus would do or say next, but none of it was irrational or arbitrary, and all of it makes sense in hindsight and has inspired the entire world for millennia. Who would not want to live and be described in this way?

This is the life that God has called each one of us to, and which is possible for every one of us if we would only cooperate with his grace and try our hardest. It may seem like a daunting task. In fact, as Pope Francis tells us, "Faith is no refuge for the fainthearted."[6] In Sacred Scripture, the Lord himself encourages us, "Take my yoke upon you, and learn from me; for I am gentle and lowly in heart, and you will find rest for your souls. For my yoke is easy, and my burden is light .... be of good cheer, I have overcome the world .... with God all things are possible" (Matthew 11:29-30; John 16:33; Matthew 19:26).

To review, this chapter has focused on the strategy of starting small by focusing on withdrawing bit by bit from our vices rather than immediately striving for great acts of virtue. This entails removing ourselves from circumstances that may tempt us, focusing on how we must act in the here and now, and reflecting on how our vices do not lead to true happiness. We looked at four stages of growth in virtue, what separates each stage, and what a person should focus on in each stage in order to make progress toward the next. The following chapter presents a strategy that should complement this one; it will show how the virtues are connected to one another, and how we can use this reality to our advantage to make quicker progress in moral growth.

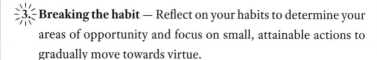

Strategies

1. Fake it till you make it.

2. Overshoot the target.

3. **Breaking the habit** — Reflect on your habits to determine your areas of opportunity and focus on small, attainable actions to gradually move towards virtue.

4

Know Thyself

I grew up a picky eater, so the food that I enjoyed, I really enjoyed. This would naturally present problems whenever I was at a party or out to dinner with friends. Since there was less food that I enjoyed, I wanted more of the food that I liked. However, taking more of it meant that there would be less for everyone else. Fortunately, I was aware that I would eat every mozzarella stick if given the chance or would surely take the last of the chocolate chip cookies. In these moments my sense of justice would come to the rescue. My conviction that everyone deserved a chance to enjoy all the food would hold me back from taking too much for myself. In time, I have learned greater temperance and have expanded my palette, such that these situations are mostly things of the past. But I have kept with me the knowledge that justice comes more easily to me than temperance, and I can use that to my advantage. This self-knowledge has helped me at various times when I have faced temptations to intemperance.

The ancient maxim "Know thyself" has endured through the ages, from the writings of ancient Greek philosophers such as Plato, to medieval theologians like Peter Abelard, to more recent thinkers like Benjamin Franklin. It is a common theme today for people to try to "find themselves." The Second Vatican Council teaches that only "Christ ... fully reveals man to man himself."[7] This is simply a restatement of what the Scriptures already reveal: "Before I formed you in the womb I knew you" (Jeremiah 1:5).

The previous chapter stressed the importance of knowing morality, of truly understanding why certain actions are good, in order to progress from vice to virtue. The strategy for this chapter also looks at knowledge, but this time knowledge of oneself. As such, we will need to return to the discussion of natural dispositions. In chapter three, we mentioned self-knowledge in the context of identifying the vices that we need to withdraw from. In this chapter, we will look at self-knowledge in respect to the moral strengths and good habits that we already possess and explain how we can use these strengths to an even greater advantage.

This strategy relies upon two concepts that St. Thomas Aquinas articulates in his moral writings: the connection of the virtues and the equality of the virtues. In short, the strategy entails *focusing on virtues that we already possess in order to strengthen our weaker virtues or the virtues we lack.*

Most often, a person's intuition leads him to attempt growth in virtue by working directly at eliminating his vices by means of practicing the contrary virtues, using strategies like the ones we have discussed up to this point. While this can be helpful, it can also be difficult to "start from scratch" with a virtue we have never really practiced. Further, if we do not meet with immediate success or experience great failure, it can be easy to give up.

The advantage of this chapter's strategy is that we do not have to start from scratch; instead, we begin with good habits that we have already cultivated and focus on increasing these habits to strengthen our weaker good habits. In order to explain this strategy, we will have to investigate how the virtues are connected.

Objections to Virtue Connectivity

There have been varying opinions about the idea of virtue connectivity throughout time. In short, the concept is that, just as a human is made up of all different parts (limbs, organs, bones, etc.) that are connected to make one body, so also the virtues are different character traits that are connected to make one overarching character. And just as good health or illness in one part of the body affects the health of other parts of the body, so also the strength or weakness of individual virtues affects the strength of the other virtues.

Some contemporary authors have denied that the virtues are connected by appealing to common experience, where a person appears to have some vices along with some virtues. However, they tend to redefine a virtue as merely a "good character trait" to raise this objection. As we saw in the previous chapter, the Catholic theory of virtue can account for good character traits that are not yet fully virtuous, namely continent habits. However, as this chapter will show, if someone truly possesses one virtue, she will also possess the other virtues.

To understand how to put virtue connectivity to work for us in building virtue, it is important to clearly state exactly what this theory means. It can be stated both positively and negatively.

Positively, the connectivity of the virtues refers to the fact that, if a person possesses one virtue, then she already possesses them all. This principle is based on the fact that virtue integrates all the capacities of the soul (reason, will, and emotions) such that they work in harmony, as we have seen. Recall that the hallmark of virtue is to act with ease, promptness, and enjoyment. In other words, the person experiences no conflict of will, can intuit how to act based on prior deliberation, and enjoys performing good acts. All the soul's capacities are united in a beautiful manifestation of human excellence.

Here is where virtue connectivity comes to light. If the intellect, will, and emotions are in harmony—and prudence perfects the intellect, justice perfects the will, and fortitude and temperance perfect the emotions—then prudence, justice, fortitude, and temperance must all be connected. Therefore, if a person possesses one virtue, then she possesses them all.

That is the positive expression of the concept. The same concept can be expressed negatively: in order to possess one virtue, a person must possess all the virtues. Or, stated differently, if a person lacks one virtue, he therefore lacks all the virtues.

At first, this can sound very discouraging. We are all aware of shortcomings in our moral life; does this mean we have no virtue? However, we should avoid despairing. First, we can still achieve strong moral character apart from full virtue; we do this by acquiring continence. Second, there are other ways, by grace, that we can achieve true virtue (more on this in chapter six). Third, we can use the connection of the virtues to our advantage in order to make greater and perhaps faster growth in virtue.

The connection of the virtues means that rather than having to focus on eliminating a particular vice and potentially face repeated failures, a person can focus instead on increasing a good habit that she already possesses. As that habit increases, so will all the other good habits along with it. For example, as a young picky eater I focused on increasing my justice in order to increase my temperance. Thus, we can focus on a character trait that we already excel at and simply focus on becoming better at it in order to overcome our other vices.

Illustrating the Negative Side

On the one hand, it may sound too good to be true that we can strengthen all our virtues by focusing on the ones we have already acquired. On the other hand, it may sound unbelievable that an individual cannot possess any virtues unless he possesses them all. We have already explained the principles behind why this must be the case, given what a virtue is and how it integrates the capacities of the soul. Now, to bring this concept to life, let's look at some examples.

We can find a classic example of how lacking one virtue leads to lacking other virtues in the Gospel account of King Herod, who put St. John the Baptist to death. Though the story is familiar, it is worth reading the passage again:

> For Herod had seized John and bound him and put him in prison, for the sake of Herodias, his brother Philip's wife; because John said to him, "It is not lawful for you to have her." And though he wanted to put him to death, he feared the people, because they held him to be a prophet. But when Herod's birthday came, the daughter of Herodias danced before the company, and pleased Herod, so that he promised with an oath to give her whatever she might ask. Prompted by her mother, she said, "Give me the head of John the Baptist here on a platter." And the king was sorry, but because of his oaths and his guests he commanded it to be given;

he sent and had John beheaded in the prison, and his head was
brought on a platter and given to the girl, and she brought it to her
mother (Matthew 14:3-11).

In this passage, Herod has John imprisoned because John told him that his
marriage was unlawful—because his brother, Philip, was still alive. Whether
Herodias divorced Philip or not, Herod committed adultery (see Jesus' rejection
of divorce in Matthew 19:1-12). This means that we can already identify an act
of lust on Herod's part, which likely was not an isolated act but came about
from a vice of lust. As Jesus teaches in Matthew 5:27-30, adultery comes
from lust already present in the heart. Aside from this lust, however, Herod
does seem to display some virtues at first glance. For one, he keeps his oath;
secondly, he honors his wife. Upon closer inspection, however, we will find
that his lack of one virtue makes these acts vicious as well (see chapter five
for more on false virtue).

Herod's vice of lust is confirmed by his response to his niece's dance. It must
have been some dance for him to be willing to give her even up to half of his
kingdom, as he is quoted saying in the parallel passage of Mark 6:23! It is likely
that his irrational emotions clouded his judgment. We know that he probably
possessed lust, a vice opposed to temperance, but if he lacked temperance
in one respect, he probably lacked it in another. Considering Herod was
celebrating with guests, it is likely that he was also drunk. His lustful desire
and drunkenness, therefore, so consumed him that they prevented him from
acting prudently. He spoke without thinking (rashness) and made a remarkably
foolish oath. Imagine if his niece did ask for half of his kingdom, and Herod
would have needed to explain to Caesar why a young girl now ruled over half
of his tetrarchy!

His lust led to imprudence. But it did not end there. When his niece made her
request for the head of John the Baptist, he granted it. On one level, this seems
to be an act of justice: Herod kept his oath, and as king, he had the authority to
put a prisoner to death. However, Mark's Gospel provides a significant detail
that Matthew omits: "Herod feared John, knowing that he was a righteous and
holy man, and kept him safe. When he heard him, he was much perplexed;
and yet he heard him gladly" (Mark 6:20). This passage reveals that Herod

knew John was innocent, and that he was entertained by listening to John. It is unjust to put an innocent person to death, and Herod's apparent remorse was not because he loved John but because he loved being entertained by him. Thus, his lust led to imprudence, which then led to injustice.

But why did Herod keep his oath? Because of his guests! This is no image of a man who stood up against persecutors for the sake of justice but rather of a coward who looked only to save face rather than save an innocent man. Due to his irrational fear, Herod was unable to remain firmly in the good—he also lacked courage.

What we see, then, in the case of Herod, is a tragic example of the unraveling of every virtue because of a lack of one. Hopefully, our failures are not as dramatic or spectacular. The point is to illustrate with an extreme example what goes on in our own lives on a smaller scale, when a lack of virtue prevents us from truly possessing the other virtues. Take a few examples that may be more relevant to our times.

A woman is in a serious dating relationship. One night, the couple is spending time with mutual friends. During the night, her boyfriend admits something embarrassing, and the group ridicules him for it, to a point that goes beyond playfulness. Although the woman sees that her boyfriend is hurt, she joins in on the ridiculing out of fear that if she does not, her friends will pick on her. In this case, her lack of courage leads to a lack of justice.

Another example: A man is asked by his neighbor for help installing a garage door opener on Friday evening so that he can surprise his wife for her birthday on Saturday when she gets back from a trip. The man agrees, knowing that he has some of his own extra work that he needs to finish for his job that week, but figuring that it is only Wednesday, and he will have the work completed by Friday and thus be available to help. That night, when he arrives home from work, he is too exhausted to do his extra work and instead watches Netflix, getting hooked on a new show. He thinks about the show all day Thursday, and when he gets home decides he will watch one episode and then finish his work. Four episodes later, he is exhausted and goes to bed, deciding to skip lunch on Friday to get his extra work done. Unfortunately, Friday he gets bogged down with extra phone calls and meetings and cannot finish the extra work. He calls his neighbor and apologizes that he cannot help with the project, and so the neighbor is not able to give the surprise to his wife. Here, a lack of temperance and self-control leads to a lack of justice—he fails to deliver on his promise. If he had not procrastinated by watching so much television, he would have had the time to help his neighbor.

Equality of the Virtues

Undoubtedly, we could find many examples of how lacking one virtue leads to the inability to act on other virtues. We all have experience of this through occasions of incontinence, but it may also be a more serious and habitual pattern. Rather than focus on proving what we have all experienced, wouldn't it be more constructive to show how we can use the connection of the virtues to our advantage? Again, the claim is that, if all the virtues are connected, then not only will lacking one virtue prevent us from fully possession the other virtues, but more importantly, growing in one virtue will cause us to grow in all of the virtues.

In order to best use this strategy, we must again consider our natural dispositions that we discussed in chapter three. We all come into this world with different temperaments and a variety of inclinations toward certain virtues and toward certain vices. Part of "knowing thyself" entails reflecting on what our natural dispositions are, since these are the foundation from which the virtues grow. We are each naturally disposed toward some virtues and not others. But, when we grow in any virtue, we will grow somewhat in all of them.

St. Thomas Aquinas uses the analogy of a hand when describing our growth in virtues. A hand is made up of five digits, each of a different length. When the human person is formed in the womb and then continues to grow into adulthood, this hand and its digits all grow together. It is not the case that first the thumb grows, and when it reaches its full length then the index finger begins to grow, and only when it is fully grown does the middle finger begin to grow, etc. Neither is it the case that all our fingers grow until they are the same length. Instead, all our fingers grow simultaneously, but they grow proportionately.

With only rare exceptions, the middle finger grows to be the longest, the pinky finger is the shortest, but all the digits reach their full length at the same time.

Similarly, good habits are of varying levels of strength in us, and they will always remain at those varied levels. Some people are naturally inclined toward courage but not to justice. Their courage will always be stronger than their justice, even if they focus on growing in justice and have great success. Just as our fingers grow in proportion, so also our virtues grow in proportion.

This means that, whatever vice you struggle with most will be the one that you always struggle with most, short of a miracle of grace. Likewise, whatever virtue comes most easily for you will always come most easily for you. It is not the case that we will "max out" on a given virtue and it will cease to grow while the other virtues catch up until they are all equal. It may appear that we experience great growth in one virtue and only small growth in another, but that is likely because the move from a vice, incontinence, or continence to virtue looks more dramatic than a virtue that simply becomes more virtuous.

St. Thomas calls this concept the "equality of the virtues," again, not in the sense that all our virtues are or can be equal in strength, but that they grow together by equal proportion. It is the principle that underlies our strategy of focusing on our stronger habits to help increase our weaker habits. Without this understanding, it may seem like a waste of time to focus on a virtue we already have rather than a virtue that we are lacking. However, if this principle is true (and it has been accepted as true in the Church for almost a millennium), then we can make as much progress by working on a virtue that we already have as working on a virtue that we do not. In fact, the claim here is that we may have greater success.

But how do we know when we have finally attained a virtue? When is that first moment when virtue is achieved, if it is true that our habits grow by equal proportion? The short answer is, we cannot know. But perhaps this is unimportant, for at any moment when we can say, for example, that someone is just, we will also be able to say that she is courageous. To illustrate this point, let us imagine something fantastical. Imagine you are standing on a giant rainbow, that is not only miles long from end to end but also miles wide.

You are standing in the yellow section and you want to walk to the end of the red section so you can peer over the side. As you walk, you stare at the rainbow beneath you and try to find that first step you will make into red, because then you will know you are almost at the end. But what you discover is that you cannot identify the first step into red. At some point, you are pretty sure that you have left orange, but you are not quite sure if you have reached red. After some time, you can look back and definitively decide that you are now in red, but you cannot figure out the moment when that happened.

This is like our growth in virtue. We may not be able to identify the precise moment when someone becomes continent, or when someone acquires a virtue, but at some point, we can definitively say that a person is continent, or does possess a virtue. We can see in hindsight what cannot be observed in the present.

We can extend the analogy further: Our habits grow in equal proportion, even if some lag others. That means that by the time we can affirm that we truly possess one virtue, we also possess the other virtues. Imagine that you are not alone on the rainbow, but a friend is standing a short distance behind you in the green section. You both start walking for red at the same pace and thereby remain the same distance apart. Because of the difficulty in discerning between reddish-orange and solid red, you will not know for sure that you are standing in red until your friend also is standing in red, even though your friend is some distance behind you. In this sense, you both reached red at the same time. Likewise, by the time we have attained any virtue, we have also attained the rest, because they all grow in equal proportion, and we are unable to identify that "first moment" when we possess one of them.

Illustrating the Positive Side

If the virtues are connected and proportional, how, then, can we use this to our advantage? Just as we looked at negative examples to prove virtue connectivity, it will be helpful to take positive examples of how working on a strong habit can help to strengthen weaker habits. I have had success with this strategy. Before I was married, I was living in a mostly unfinished rental unit because the rent was cheap, and I wanted to save as much money as I could. When I say mostly unfinished, there was plumbing and a way to cook meals, but the floor was bare concrete, the ceiling was missing half of its tiles (and the tiles over the shower caved in halfway through my time there), there were doors without doorframes, and the cinderblock walls were bare. That would have been fine for a short time, except for the fact that I also had to spray a bug barrier around the perimeter on a regular basis to keep out the centipedes and cockroaches, as well as set traps for the mice.

While it took a while the first few nights to fall asleep, I eventually settled into my circumstances. At least the bug barrier worked (except against spiders) and the mice were infrequent visitors. But, one day, I had quite a fright when I sat on my bed, tying my shoelaces, only to look down and find a neon green spider sitting on the bed right in front of me. That part was not so bad; I brushed him off and stepped on him. But during this action, I noticed something strange on my shirt, which upon closer inspection I discovered was a nest that the spider had made! I whipped off my shirt and threw it across the room, wondering how that could have happened, and then quickly rushed to my other shirts—which were hanging in the middle of my room on a standing clothes rack because there was no closet—to inspect them all for spider nests. Thankfully, I found none, and then I turned back to the shirt on the floor. What should I do?

When I told friends about this story, they unanimously responded that they would have either thrown out the shirt or burned it, psychologically unable to ever wear it again. A large part of me wanted to do the same, but I knew that would be irrational. The spider was dead; the spider nest was destroyed; there was no reason not to wear the shirt again ... right? I recognized that, while it was legitimate to feel some fear when I first found the spider and nest, it was irrational to continue to fear wearing the shirt.

I was determined to conquer this irrational fear, but I could not do so by directly aiming for courage. If I were to conquer my fear by aiming directly for courage, I would have to wear the shirt right then and there, which I could not bring myself to do. How, then, could I conquer the fear? I focused instead on prudence, on reasoning with myself that it was safe to wear the shirt. But I really had to understand that, and this took some time—as well as washing the shirt at least twice, inspecting the shirt every day, and keeping it separate from the rest of my clothes. After several weeks, I had finally convinced myself that there was truly no danger in wearing the shirt; I had managed to perceive the situation clearly and internalized the truth of the matter. While I made no progress in overcoming my fear through striving for courage directly, I was still able to grow in courage and properly moderate my fear by focusing on prudence and increasing my right reason regarding the shirt.

That is one example of how the connectivity of the virtues can be used to our advantage. We can work on our stronger habits in order to increase our weaker habits. For me, my prudence was stronger than my courage, and I was able to increase my courage by increasing my prudence. They grew in equal proportion. But there can be countless other examples.

Perhaps a person struggles with social courage and seeks at all costs to avoid confrontation. She witnesses a coworker getting harassed by a supervisor but remains quiet out of fear of confrontation. Her conscience pulls at her because she knows that she should do something, but the fear paralyzes her. Instead of focusing on acting courageously, she can focus on justice. If justice is a stronger virtue for her, she can focus on what she owes to her coworker, who is hurt and has no one else to defend her. Focusing on justice and her duty to defend her coworker, she overcomes her fear and confronts the supervisor, or instead schedules a meeting with someone higher up the chain.

Another example woud be someone who struggles with lust. Perhaps he had a history of viewing pornography, and although he has since stopped, he still regularly catches himself having lustful fantasies and ogles women in public. He has had little success in simply willing himself to be chaste and to stop acting lustfully. Instead, he turns to justice, a stronger virtue for him, and focuses on what he owes to other women. He recognizes that he owes respect to each woman, not to treat them as objects for his gratification, to focus on what they have to say in conversations. Whenever he encounters an attractive woman, he reminds himself what he owes her, and little by little he is able to resist any fantasies and ogling. He begins winning small victories, which become larger victories, until eventually he has broken the habit of lust and no longer needs to remind himself how to act; he now simply acts appropriately. By working on increasing in justice, he was able to increase in chastity.

An Alternate Method

There is one more aspect of the connection of the virtues that provides an alternative method for this chapter's strategy. Not only are all the virtues connected with each other, they are also connected within themselves. Recall how chapter two explained that there are four cardinal virtues, but all other virtues are sub-virtues or parts of the cardinal virtues. This explains how, when someone possesses courage, she will also possess patience and perseverance as sub-virtues of courage.

However, St. Thomas also writes of "species" of a virtue—in other words, different domains in which a virtue can be applied. For example, *temperance* is the virtue of properly moderating our desires. When temperance is applied to food, we call it *abstinence*; when it is applied to drinking, it is called *sobriety*; when it is applied to sex, it is called *chastity*. Moderation in drinking presents different challenges from moderation in eating or with the sexual appetite.

Likewise, with the other cardinal virtues St. Thomas divides the species of prudence into general prudence, domestic prudence, military prudence, and leadership prudence. What they all have in common is the habit of seeing situations rightly, prioritizing correctly, and commanding the will to right action, but each manifests in a different enough way that they can be considered different species. While there are many similarities among them, one does not, for example, run a country exactly the way one runs a family, or run a family exactly the way one runs a military.

The claim here is that someone does not fully possess the cardinal virtue until he possesses all its parts and species. One person may eat moderately but drink excessively, for example, and so he does not yet possess true temperance. Think of how we are one body made up of various systems (skeletal system, muscular system, digestive system, nervous system, etc.), and those systems are also made up of various parts. Health of the body requires health of all the various systems, and the health of each system requires the health of the parts within the systems. Likewise, the virtuous person must possess the virtues, but the virtues are only possessed if their sub-virtues and species also are. This connection among the species of the virtue, like the overall connection of the virtues, can be used to our advantage.

The most common examples of how we can put this connection to use typically have to do with temperance. If someone is struggling to maintain a diet (and scientific studies have supported the success of this strategy), she should focus on other areas of temperance, such as getting the right amount of sleep, falling asleep and waking at consistent times, maintaining a strict schedule so there are not gaps to be filled with eating, incorporating some form of exercising, and enjoying periods of true relaxation as opposed to laziness or procrastination. Facing a diet head-on can be very difficult but strengthening other areas of temperance that may come to the person more easily can help with the diet. And similar to what happens with inter-virtue connectivity, the weaker species of a virtue will strengthen proportionately as the stronger species strengthen.

For example, those who struggle with pornography often have a lot of time to themselves when they can view it. To overcome this, they should be sure to eat and sleep well each day (so one is not as tired and susceptible to temptation), exercise regularly (as an outlet for tension and growth in self-respect), and keep a stricter schedule (to avoid long stretches of free time alone). The saints have also recommended fasting as a sure way to combat temptations. For maximum effect, this strategy can be employed along with some of the others in this book: Always begin any time on the computer or smartphone with prayer (see chapter six), perhaps exchange a smartphone for one without Internet capability, or at least uninstall problematic applications to withdraw from the occasions for the vice (see chapter three), and possibly install software that allows a trusted friend to keep you accountable for the websites you view (see chapter five).

The connection of the virtues may be the biggest secret of virtue ethics, but one that should not be a secret. Whenever I have taught this to students, from undergraduates to permanent diaconate candidates in their forties, fifties, or sixties, they have expressed how encouraging and helpful this strategy is.

Improving a habit one already possesses seems more achievable than acquiring a habit that one does not possess, and it still achieves this along the way. This strategy, though it derives from a principle of virtue ethics that at first glance seems daunting, turns out to be encouraging and liberating. The approach has now expanded: rather than focusing on a particular habit (as the first three strategies do), this strategy incorporates the help of other habits. The last three chapters will continue to expand our efforts to incorporate the help of other people and the help of God.

Strategies

1. Fake it till you make it.

2. Overshoot the target.

3. Breaking the habit.

4. **Know thyself** — Utilize the connectivity of the virtues and continue to build upon your strong virtues to assist in the growth of your weaker ones.

5

A Friend in Need
Is a Friend Indeed

Throughout my childhood and well into college I was very skinny. Being active in multiple sports was surely a significant factor in this, but I had always thought that it was because I was a temperate eater. Remaining skinny felt effortless—in fact, I did not really give my weight any thought. If anything, I wanted to bulk up with more muscle. From my perspective, it seemed that I could eat anything, and it would have no effect on me. From others' perspective, people always marveled at how I was able to turn down desserts, breakfast pastries, or second helpings of meals.

Then I graduated from college and was living on my own for the first time. Freedom! I remember vividly the day I realized that I could decide how many chocolate chip cookies I could have, and that I could have them whenever I wanted. Surely, this was the key to happiness and the best perk of being an adult.

But one day I realized that I was eating a lot of chocolate chip cookies. In fact, I seemed to be eating throughout the whole day. And in a matter of a few short years, I was already able to look back at older photos and wonder how I was so skinny back then. I was temperate, so how could this happen?

Then it hit me—I was not temperate. I thought back to my habits as a teenager and compared them to my adult habits, and what I found was that I was never temperate at all—I was simply a picky eater. Growing up, the reason why I turned down fancy desserts and pastries was not because I knew how to eat moderately; it was because I did not like that food. It is very easy to refrain from eating something that you do not enjoy. It is much less easy to refrain from eating something that you very much enjoy. And that was the problem that I now faced: the difference between then and now was that now I could eat whatever I wanted whenever I wanted, and I had not developed the habit of doing so in moderation.

What appeared to be temperance in my early years was a happy combination of high metabolism, exercise, and a picky palette. But now, with the metabolism fading, no sports coach to make me exercise, and the freedom to eat what I wanted, I realized that I never had the virtue at all. I only had a façade of virtue, what theologians call false virtue or a mere semblance of virtue. All it took to reveal it was a mere change in circumstances, and the mask of virtue was removed.

Held Accountable

False virtue is a real problem in the moral life. Not only do we not want to be deceived by others who feign true virtue, but we also want to ensure that we are developing true virtue and not masquerading vices. However, it can be very difficult to see our own habits as they truly are.

As we saw in chapter two, we tend to view our habits as virtues, even if they are vices, and to perceive true virtue as an extreme. For this reason, a great strategy in the moral life is to find an accountability partner, that is, someone who can mercifully identify our faults and continuously encourage us to pursue right actions.

We have surely heard at one time or another a man introducing his wife and saying, "She keeps me honest." While the statement is made in jest, it is a fact that true friends make us better people. Friendship involves willing the good of another person, so a true friend will always look to help us improve, rather than dragging us down into his own vices. A true friend is willing to have the uncomfortable conversations and to privately admonish us when we go astray, because fraternal correction is a spiritual work of mercy—a true act of love.

But we are lucky to find one friend who is willing to suffer with us in our trials, rejoice with us in our victories, and to motivate us to aspire higher, let alone many friends like this. The ideal situation is to make a true friend who truly wills our good, but I cannot give advice on how to find such a friend outside of praying for one.

Fortunately, the strategy for this chapter can be pursued even without such deeply caring friends. We know all too well how ready people are to point out another's faults. The saying, "Every time you point your finger, three more point back at you" expresses how we are more ready to point out others' faults than our own (and how we usually blame others for the very faults that we possess). Jesus put it more dramatically when he said, "Why do you see the speck that is in your brother's eye, but do not notice the log that is in your own eye? ... first take the log out of your own eye, and then you will see clearly to take the speck out of your brother's eye" (Matthew 7:3, 5).

Ideally, we find a person who has removed the log out of their own eye so that they can help us with our log. But, even if we cannot, we can still use the fallen eagerness of others to point out our faults to our advantage. If we can find someone with a good level of dependability, we can confide in him the vices we are trying to eliminate or the virtues we are trying to acquire and ask for his help. Of course, we should use discernment, as we do not want to make ourselves vulnerable to someone who may not have our good at heart.

If a good friend or reliable acquaintance cannot be found, the saints have urged finding a spiritual director or a regular confessor. Such individuals are gifted at assessing our spiritual strengths and weaknesses and have no stake in embarrassing us in front of others, which can make it easier to confide in them.

Whether our accountability partner is a priest, friend, parent, spouse, or stranger, there are many advantages to having such a partner who will help us progress more quickly toward virtue. First, another person may be able to perceive faults in us that we have become blinded to. For instance, a friend may point out that we always assume we are right and never consider other people's opinions, or that we are excessively harsh in our speech toward a specific person. Conversely, another person may also be able to point out good habits in us that we take for granted or have not noticed, such as the way in which we are well-organized, or the fact that we listen well to other people. Pointing out our faults can help us to pursue the strategy of slowly withdrawing from our vices (from chapter three). Pointing out our good habits can help us in pursuing the strategy of strengthening one virtue in order to strengthen all of them (from chapter four).

A second advantage to having an accountability partner is this: an accountability partner can motivate us to continue to strive to eliminate a particular vice or acquire a particular virtue. If we tell our partner to draw to our attention, for example, every time we gossip, our inner shame and embarrassment will drive us to want to prevent our partner from having to point these occasions out, which will inspire us to try harder. In my experience, the fact that I do not want to have to confess a particular sin again has been good motivation for trying harder to avoid it.

The partner's intervention can be more or less overt, depending on the urgency of the situation. You could ask the partner to do anything from privately notify us when we fall into bad habits to publicly pointing out when we act wrongly, depending on what will motivate us better. I remember an old classmate who wanted to stop using foul language. He asked his buddy to punch him in the arm any time he swore. After a week and some pretty large bruises, he switched to having to put a quarter in a jar every time he swore. Whatever it takes (within reason) to eliminate the vice! As Jesus graphically warned, "It is better that you lose one of your members than that your whole body be thrown into hell" (Matthew 5:29).

In order to make good use of an accountability partner, however, both our partner and ourselves need to know how to identify good and evil acts, and to be able to discern true from false virtue. We do not want our partner steering us away from virtue and into vice! For this reason, it is important to review how moral actions are evaluated. The following sections will explore the elements that make up a moral act and how to evaluate them. This will then allow us to return to the concept of false virtue and see how our accountability partner can help us.

Moral Object

When it comes to the moral evaluation of our actions, the Church teaches us that there are three pieces that make up a moral act, and therefore three aspects that need to be evaluated. A human action consists of a *moral object*, an *intention*, and accompanying *circumstances*. Let us explain each part in turn before looking at how they are to be evaluated.

The first piece of an act is what the person chooses. "Moral object" may seem like a strange term, but there are two good reasons for using it. First, a moral object is different from a moral subject, or moral agent. We are moral subjects. Of all creation, is only human beings that can properly be called moral agents, because only we act with reason and free choice. The moral subject is the agent, that is, the person performing some action, so the moral object is what the person chooses in her action.

There is another reason why this aspect of our actions is called a "moral object." The object is only part of the act. In addition to the object, the person's act is composed of an intention, and circumstances, too. So, the object is not synonymous with the whole moral act—it is only a part of the act. The object is some activity that is chosen by the acting subject (the person), but we will not be able to fully identify what the moral act is until we know what the person's intention is for choosing that object.

Although the intention and circumstances are distinct from the object of an action, the object is not a mere physical description of some behavior. We do not say that the man moved his arm but that he threw a punch. We do not say that the woman flailed her legs but that she swam. The man did not just pick up a wallet; he stole it. The woman did not just spin; she danced. A mere physical description of an act is morally unintelligible. Why? First, because we could continue to re-describe all these activities in more and more reductive ways, until we describe them all as simply synapses firing in the brain. But this does not help us at all in moral evaluation. An alleged murderer would not present a good case by simply claiming, "I didn't shoot the man; I just pulled my finger" or "I didn't kill the man; a synapse just fired in my brain!" A mere physical description is amoral and could be re-described until it is described away.

This leads to the second reason why a mere description would be morally unintelligible. A physical description of an action devoid of context is random, but people do not act randomly. Instead, people always act for a purpose. We choose certain activities because they have some meaning in and of themselves that we see as getting us closer to a goal that we have. Another way of putting this is that we choose certain moral objects because we see them as conducive to achieving our intentions.

If we choose certain moral objects over others, it is because we view them as more conducive to our ultimate goals. But if moral objects can be "choice worthy" or not, that is, reasonable or not, then they can already be morally evaluated even before considering our further goals. While some objects may always be wrong to choose, most objects are morally neutral in the abstract. In these cases, we will also need to evaluate the person's intention in choosing the object to get the correct moral evaluation. To return to the above examples, attacking, swimming, and dancing are all moral objects chosen for some reason, but without knowing that reason—that is, intention—we still will not have all that we need to morally evaluate the act. There could be many different intentions that lead someone to attack, swim, or dance, and these intentions themselves could be good or bad. The man could have thrown a punch because he was in a drunken rage, or because he was practicing martial arts. The woman could have been swimming to win an Olympic race or to escape from a swarm of bees. The woman could have danced as a form of exercise or to seduce her boss. The moral object is chosen because it has some inherent meaning that the person sees as a means to achieving her further goal and intention. To make a complete evaluation, we then need to consider the person's intention.

Intention

The meaning of the term *intention* is straightforward. Sometimes, theologians will refer to an intention as the "end" of an act—that is, the goal of the act. It is the greater, overarching reason why we choose a particular moral object. Not only do we choose moral objects because of their inherent meaning and orientation, but we also choose them as a means to some end, or as a path to achieving some goal. Thus, the intention is distinct but closely related to the moral object, and both must be evaluated.

It is worth noting that, while most theoretical ethical examples are set up to have one moral object and one intention, it is common for people to have more than one intention when performing an action. For example, a person performing on stage may do so to make a living, to have fun, and to brag about her success to her friends. These could be multiple intentions for choosing the object of public performance. Typically, though, even when there seem to be multiple intentions, there is one primary intention that drives the action and under which the other intentions fall.

Sometimes these secondary intentions are better described as beneficial consequences rather than proper intentions. However, if a person did act with more than one intention, each intention would need to be evaluated separately. In the example of our performer, her act would be good insofar as she intended to make an honest living and enjoy herself, but immoral insofar as she intended to boast about her skill. This is helpful to realize as we look at our own actions.

We also need to clarify that a foreseen consequence of an action is not the same thing as an intention. There are many times throughout a day when we may act for some goal while regretting that some other consequence may follow, but this does not mean that we intend or will those regrettable consequences. For example, a parent may see that he needs to discipline his child for her misbehavior, and so he chooses to ground her. The parent may foresee that in grounding his child she will become angry and cry, but this is a consequence beside his intention, not his actual intention. His intention is to correct his daughter so that she will learn to be well-behaved, not to emotionally hurt her. Thus, the intention here is to lovingly correct, not to cause emotional pain, even if he suspects that that may likely ensue.

There are all sorts of occasions where this may occur: wanting to praise someone but recognizing that others could feel jealousy; wanting to stay up late but knowing it could exacerbate one's illness; wanting to take a child to the grocery store but knowing that it will expose him to lewd images on magazines in the checkout line. We likely encounter hundreds of these situations every day, simply because we live in a fallen world where there is a lot of good and bad.

If we were to avoid everything that could potentially lead to a bad outcome, we would avoid doing a lot of good in the world. Many of these outcomes are out of our control, especially when it comes to other people's emotions. We sometimes simply cannot help the way a person will react to our action, and while we should be mindful of our effect on others (as St. Paul teaches us in 1 Corinthians 8), we cannot let this prevent us from doing great works.

How do we judge whether or how to act in these situations? First, we can determine whether some consequence is intended by us or not by asking ourselves a simple question: Would I still perform this activity if that consequence would not happen? For example, if I would not discipline my daughter unless it made her cry, then that means I am intending to cause her emotional harm. But if my hope is that she will take the discipline reasonably and not cry, that means I am intending the correction and not the emotional harm. If I am intending some evil effect, then I should refrain from the action.

Second, we need to weigh the good effect of our intention with the potential bad effects that we foresee. Was my daughter's misbehavior only a slight matter and the discipline would cause more emotional pain than helpful correction? Perhaps I should only talk to her and omit the punishment. Is my child so distracted by his new toy that he likely will not even look at the magazines at checkout? Then it is probably safe to take him to the grocery store.

In the end, we must make a judgment call. This is why the virtue of prudence is so important. An accountability partner can help us by listening if we need to talk something out or by helping us see if we are not being honest with ourselves about what we are intending to do.

It is challenging to weigh good and bad effects against each other because there is no unit of measurement we can use like inches or gallons. We will not be able to scrutinize the situation with scientific accuracy because every situation presents a unique set of circumstances, and even if we could we often would not have the time to. While we should reflect on our decisions before and after making them (more on this in chapter seven), we cannot allow reflection to prevent us from acting altogether. We make a decision, learn from it, and try to improve in future decisions.

This is not to say that our decisions do not matter, or that there is no objective right and wrong in our particular circumstances. How to evaluate our decisions will be discussed below. For now, it is important to remember that an accountability partner can point out patterns in our decision-making, or to point out when we do not follow through with our resolve to change these patterns. Such a partner can help us ensure that our intentions are good and that we are choosing good moral objects for the right reasons.

Circumstances

We do not act in a vacuum. We act within a set of circumstances. While the moral object and intention together make up the essence of a moral act, the accompanying circumstances are a variety of details that contextualize the act. There could be countless circumstances, such as when the act was performed, to whom it was performed, by what means it was performed, where it was performed, or how it was performed.

Often, most of these circumstances are not important when it comes to evaluating an act. For example, if someone gives money to charity, it does not much matter what time of the day he sent the money, or what pen he used to sign the check. Sometimes, though, circumstances can be more relevant to the evaluation, such as if an employer reprimands his employee privately or publicly, if an apartment tenant listens to loud music during the day or in the middle of the night, or if a teenager performs his chores dutifully or lazily.

As we will soon see, even these circumstances do not change the overall evaluation of an act, but they can decrease or increase how good or bad it is. Consideration of the circumstances of an act, then, is important for the attainment of virtue.

To fully reach that virtuous mean of action, the circumstances must be right to produce a most perfect action. For example, while it may be morally right to be angry at certain things (such as injustices and atrocities), truly virtuous anger requires being angry to the right degree, at the right time, toward the right person, and for the right duration. It is very difficult to get this right! However, the circumstances do provide us with a handy checklist for how we can improve.

Perhaps we got angry at the right thing and to the right degree, but we remained angry for too long and harbored unforgiveness. Now we know that duration is the circumstance that we need to work on. Perhaps instead we got angry at the wrong person; now we know that "who" is the circumstance we need to work on. Recognizing these circumstances can help us as we ask an accountability partner to help us work on these things.

Occasionally, a circumstance is so relevant to the type of action we perform that it is not considered a circumstance at all, but instead a detail that helps us to more accurately identify the correct moral object of the action. For example, killing is a bare physical description. Animals kill, hurricanes kill, and viruses kill, but none of these is a moral agent. "Killing," then, is not a true moral object. However, murder, lethal self-defense, capital punishment, vigilantism, and fighting in war are all types of killing that are considered separate moral objects. They all share the physical act of killing, but what differentiates them is not merely a circumstance. It is not circumstantial whether someone kills an innocent victim or an unjust aggressor, nor is it merely circumstantial whether someone takes it upon himself to kill a criminal or is deputized by the government to kill a criminal for the preservation of the common good and security of the state.

Likewise, sex is a bare physical description of an act that even nonrational animals can perform. When we distinguish between the marital act, fornication, adultery, and rape, it is not merely circumstantial whether one's sexual partner is one's spouse or another's spouse, or whether the other person has given consent or not. In both examples, we see that what may appear to be a circumstance is so rationally relevant and important to the moral object that is chosen that it is not a circumstance at all but rather a specification of the moral object. Thus, all these examples are examples of different moral objects. Although they may all share "killing" or "sex" as physical descriptions, they can be evaluated differently.

Evaluating Moral Acts

We now understand the three parts that make up a moral act. Now what? It is no good to know what a hammer and a screwdriver are if you do not know how to use them. Likewise, it does not help us to know the parts of a moral act unless we know how to use them to make us virtuous. In other words, we need to be able to evaluate them, to know when they are good or evil and thereby make us virtuous or vicious. While an accountability partner may be able to give us advice, we want to make sure that his advice is sound! Even if we sometimes struggle with evaluating acts correctly, we need to at least know the basics of how to evaluate them to make sure our partners are giving reasonable advice.

Throughout the ages, there have been many philosophers and schools of ethics that have only focused on one of these three parts, but the Church has always taught that all three must be evaluated—and they must be evaluated in a particular order. First, the moral object of an action must be evaluated because it has meaning in and of itself—which is why the act was chosen at all; it can be evaluated on its own even before considering one's intentions or the present circumstances. In the abstract, a moral object can be morally good, neutral, or evil (although, practically speaking, whenever an object is chosen it will always be good or evil—that is, it will always either contribute to or hinder the individual's flourishing and perfection).

Some objects, such as telling the truth, helping the poor, or educating a person are morally good. People may do these things for the wrong reasons, but they are still good objects. Other objects, such as picking up a stick or driving a car, are morally neutral, and we would need more information to discern why a person did these things or the relevant circumstances to evaluate them. Was the person picking up a stick a child who was specifically told not to pick up that stick? Or was the person picking up a stick to help clean a neighbor's yard?

Intrinsic Evils

Some moral objects, however, are always evil. The Church commonly refers to these as *intrinsic* evils, which means that they can never bring about a good goal. We certainly may try to choose these objects to bring about good, but we will never be successful. These objects are in and of themselves ordered away from true human freedom and flourishing, and thus cannot be chosen for the sake of some good. As God in his divine authority teaches us, we may not do evil that good may come of it (see Romans 3:8).

The point here is not simply that we cannot do evil that good may come of it, but that it is not possible to achieve goodness through an evil act. It simply cannot be done. If there is some good outcome as a result of our evil object, it is a happy coincidence, but not something achieved through the performance of evil.

Therefore, even if we choose an evil object with a good intention, such as euthanizing a person to end his suffering, this does not change the fact that the object is evil. The evil object means the entire action is evil and morally prohibited. In the case of euthanasia, for instance, the man's suffering is not in fact ended, but it is the man who is capable of suffering who is ended. Thus, a good is not achieved through the evil—only the evil and its aftermath.

While it is not an exhaustive list, the Church has named many intrinsic evils in order to help guide the faithful, including murder, genocide, abortion, euthanasia, suicide, mutilation, torture, coercion, arbitrary imprisonment, arbitrary deportation, slavery, and contraception.[8] Again, these moral objects are all naturally opposed to authentic human freedom and flourishing, and thus cannot possibly lead to a good outcome. For that reason, they are immoral, and no good intention can change that fact.

Intention and Circumstances

This brings us to the evaluation of one's intention. If we determine that a given moral object is intrinsically evil, the intention is not able to change it into something good. We have all heard the phrase "the road to hell is paved with good intentions." The meaning behind this adage is that a good intention cannot make an evil object good. Choosing an evil object with a good intention will still not be a good act. A good intention may lessen how evil the action is, or perhaps remove some responsibility for the evil, but it cannot change the moral evaluation. It is like having a burnt steak and trying to cover over the flavor with sauce; you can try whatever you like to mask the charring, but it is still a burnt steak underneath. At best you can only take away some of the bad taste, but the steak cannot become un-burnt by adding good condiments.

Intention plays a bigger role with a good or neutral moral object. Of course, the ideal is that someone chooses a good object with a good intention and therefore performs a morally good act. However, if I choose a good object with an evil intention, my intention renders the entire act evil. It is like having a well-cooked steak and then spoiling it in some way, whether by cooking it some more until it is burned, smothering it in a sour sauce, or freezing it. An evil intention spoils the whole action.

Why can one's intention turn good objects evil but not evil objects good? Because an evil object by nature cannot result in human excellence. It is a contradiction and logical impossibility for something that cannot bring about human excellence to be an excellent human choice by any means. If some action by nature cannot result in true human excellence, then not even God's intention could make it good.

On the other side, anything good can be spoiled by some lack. For example, going to Mass and giving to charity are good objects. However, if a politician is only going to Mass and giving to charity during election season so that he will be seen by others, in hopes that they will then vote for him, the politician is cultivating vices of vainglory, dissimulation, and hypocrisy rather than true virtues of worship, humility, and generosity. If I lack a good intention in choosing a good object, then my ultimate act will lack the full perfection of good. A good object may be naturally ordered to a good outcome, so I may happen to do some good for another person. But since I lack a good intention, I am ruining my soul in the performance of the act, and so it is considered evil.

Here, again, an accountability partner can be useful in helping us see where we may need to purify our intentions.

At this point, the circumstances may be evaluated, but since they are not essential to the type of action performed, they do not have the ability to change the overall moral evaluation from good to evil or vice versa. Instead, the circumstances can only increase or decrease the goodness of a good act or increase or decrease the evil of an evil act.

For example, in Luke 21:1-4, we see the story of rich men donating to the Temple out of their excess and a poor widow donating all that she has. All in this parable are performing a good act, but the widow's act is more perfect because she gives all that she has. With that said, if the widow were not a widow, but instead married with young children, and still gave all her money, that circumstance would severely decrease the goodness of her donation because it would be unfair to her family.

The Evaluation

As mentioned in the previous sections, the essence of a moral action rests in the object and intention, so, once these are evaluated, we have the correct evaluation of the act. We have four options: 1) a good object and good intention produce a good act; 2) a good object and evil intention produce a subjectively evil act; 3) an evil object and evil intention produce an evil act; 4) an evil object and good intention produce an evil act that may be lessened somewhat in its evil. As we can see, if there is anything morally lacking in our object or intention, we will not perform a morally good act. To be virtuous, we must choose good objects for the right reasons.

Morality of Object		Morality of Intention		Overall Morality of Act
Good	$\rightarrow$	Good	$\rightarrow$	Good
Good	$\rightarrow$	Evil	$\rightarrow$	Evil: false virtue
Evil	$\rightarrow$	Evil	$\rightarrow$	Evil
Evil	$\rightarrow$	Good	$\rightarrow$	Evil: false virtue

Uncovering False Virtues

Having explored how moral actions are evaluated, we are now in a better position to understand and identify any false virtues that we may have. True virtue consists in performing perfect acts, where the object, intention, and circumstances are all good. On the flip side, false virtue entails actions where some perfection is lacking but does not appear to be. From our analysis, the two ways that this can possibly occur are through choosing a good object with an evil intention or choosing an evil object with a good intention. While sometimes the evil in both cases is obvious, other times these acts truly give the semblance of virtue, which is where an accountability partner can help in calling us to task.

We already provided an example of the first scenario where false virtue can occur (a good object with an evil intention). This was the example of a politician who only goes to Mass during the election cycle but stops attending once he has been reelected. To a potential voter who does not attend the same church as the politician, the politician may seem to be a very pious individual, and the fact that he attends Mass may be a significant factor in voting for him. However, if he is only attending Mass precisely for this reason—to be seen by others so that they will vote for him—then he is not exercising piety but instead using the liturgy for his own goal. He is taking something that should be an end in itself and making it a means to some other end. Although getting elected may also be a good end (after all, we need good elected officials), it is here pursued by belittling and making a mockery of worship of God.

Other examples abound: the rich man who appears prudent with money but is actually stingy and miserly and acquires his wealth by defrauding others; the woman who seems like a caring shoulder to cry on but is really trying to learn secrets to gossip about; the teacher who seems so dedicated to his students but is so at the expense of being present to his own children.

We also already provided an example of the second scenario where false virtue can occur (an evil object with a good intention). This was the example of a person who advocates for euthanasia in order to end the patient's suffering. It seems merciful to want to end the suffering, but this is in fact a false mercy. Mercy entails compassion, a word that means to "suffer with." So true mercy is to be present in the patient's suffering, to suffer with the patient, and to attempt to lessen it through life-giving activities rather than a life-ending activity.

Again, examples abound: the person who advocates abortion for the sake of empowering women, although this eliminates what is unique to femininity and does so at the expense of the rights of the unborn child; the person who appears to have such a great sense of humor and is the life of the party, but only ever makes jokes at others' expense; the person who is always helping others to get out of inconvenient situations, but does so by advocating lying or by making up his own crafty lies.

A virtuous accountability partner who knows us well should be able to identify any inconsistency in our objects and intentions and bring them to light. What about if our partner cannot identify them? If we know how to evaluate our acts and can instruct our partner in what to look for, this strategy can still be a great help. The combination of having another set of eyes to observe our behavior along with our desire to succeed in the eyes of another works well to give us an extra kick in the pants to try harder.

Of course, we all do know one person who is virtuous enough to see our faults and strengths, who says, "I have called you friends" (John 15:15), who is willing to suffer with and for us to ease our burden (see Matthew 11:29–30), and who will never abandon us (see Matthew 28:20). This, of course, is Jesus. It is to the Son of God that we now turn in our next strategy.

Strategies

1. Fake it till you make it.

2. Overshoot the target.

3. Breaking the habit.

4. Know thyself.

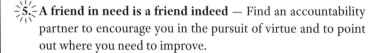 **A friend in need is a friend indeed** — Find an accountability partner to encourage you in the pursuit of virtue and to point out where you need to improve.

6

Let Go and Let God

How often in life have we said, "I wish I had known that sooner!" How often have we learned something and wished that we had been told it years earlier? Things would have gone so much more smoothly! I experienced this wish in my graduate studies, and thought that, when I became a professor, I would do my students a service by teaching them the later principles of theology right at the start in order to give them a head start. It was not long before I realized that there is a wisdom to learning things in a certain order, and that the reason we do not learn some principles or lessons early on is that we are not yet ready for them. Even if they are taught, they are not retained.

In this chapter, we come face to face with this paradox. On the one hand, the aspects of virtue presented here cannot be understood without the chapters that come before it. On the other hand, the strategy presented in this chapter is more important than any other strategy. It is the very first one that we should pursue—and, in fact, should always pursue along with all the other strategies.

What is this strategy? Simply, *pray* for virtue.

This sounds obvious but is so often overlooked. Perhaps it is overlooked because it is so obvious. How many times do we set out to accomplish something, but only pray when it goes wrong or when we cannot achieve it? We often treat God like a divine doctor who can fix things after they are already broken. But medicine should be not only about curing but also about preventing. Likewise, we often view God as the savior who saves us after our sins, but not as the savior who has saved us even before our sins.

For example, you can save a person from a hole in the ground in two different ways: either by pulling her out of the hole that she fell into, or by preventing her from falling into the hole altogether. On a large scale, the Blessed Virgin Mary is saved from sin in the second way through the grace of the Immaculate Conception, while the rest of us are saved in the first way through the sacrament of Baptism.[9] However, on a smaller scale, when it comes to our daily endeavors, there is nothing stopping us from being saved or healed or helped by God in the second way—nothing, that is, except ourselves!

God is ever ready and willing to give us the grace and help that we need to resist sin and to grow in virtue, but he will never force himself on us. He loves us too much to take away our free will. He instead waits patiently for us to ask for his help—and thank goodness he is so patient for all of the times that we forget to ask!

It is well and good to state that we should pray for virtue, but when will our prayers be answered? How will it work? While none of us knows the Divine Mind, theologians have been able to work out, based on God's revelation, some of the dynamics between virtue and grace. This chapter seeks to explain a little of the "how" of graced virtue, and, though we "do not know the day or the hour," give some advice concerning the "when."

God's Timing

While God can infuse and increase any virtue in us at any time, like a good Father, He often chooses to challenge us and aid us in acting beyond the intensity of our habits (see chapter one). I learned this lesson the hard way at a time in my life when I was praying for an increase in patience. There were many things going on in my life, ranging from big concerns like finding a wife to little concerns like having to wait extra long for a metro train while the station conducted single-track maintenance. It occurred to me that I should pray for patience so that I could keep from letting these concerns bother or distract me.

Of course, I had it in my head that I would pray for patience and overnight I would find I was no longer bothered by anything. Instead, what I found was that I was still anxious about the future, and I was still getting frustrated with the delays in the metro schedule. So, I prayed some more. But the anxiety and frustrations were still there. In fact, they seemed to increase. There was a coworker at the time who tended to get on my nerves. His voice was irritating, but it seemed to me that he would never stop talking, and while I used to see him here and there, it seemed like now I was bumping into him every time I walked down the hallway! I started to get frustrated that I was becoming less patient after my prayer and was impatient with my lack of patience!

I started concocting ideas for how I could avoid this coworker at all costs—and then it hit me. My coworker was the answer to my prayers. I had been treating prayer as if God were a genie bound to grant my every wish and was frustrated that he was not. But God had not only heard but also answered my prayer—not in the way I wanted or expected, but in the way that was truly best for me. Had he just granted me patience, I could have become proud of my patience. Instead, he granted me more opportunities to practice patience. This first revealed to me the extent of my lack of patience, which in turn humbled me and led me to depend more on God's grace. Rather than run from these obstacles, I was able to see them for the challenging opportunities that they were. I was ready to face them head-on, but this time not alone.

My prayer changed from asking God to give me patience to asking God to assist me in being patient. Rather than expecting God to do the work for me, I realized I needed to cooperate with the help that God was always offering me. God's will for me was always the same, but I needed to conform my will to his, rather than trying to conform his will to mine. God wanted patience for me even more than I wanted it for myself, but he was going to help me attain it the right way, which I could not have done apart from his grace.

Sacraments

While personal prayer is powerful, as Catholics we are blessed to be able to turn to channels of grace that Christ specifically put in place to help us as well. Since the strategy of this chapter is to pray for virtue, we would be remiss if we did not mention the greatest prayer of all—the Mass—and the other liturgical rites that we call *sacraments*. While we do not have the space to explain everything about the sacraments, we should keep a few brief points in mind.

First, the Mass is the greatest prayer. In every Mass, the priest—acting in the person of Christ—thanks the Father for sending his Son, and then offers the Son back to the Father in the Holy Spirit on our behalf. The priest is ordained to make this offering, but insofar as we are baptized in Christ and united to him we can unite ourselves with this offering, as well as unite all of our smaller offerings: our successes, strengths, joys, and desires. We can even offer the bad, such as our failures, disappointments, and weaknesses, for God can bring good out of evil and redeem all things. There is no greater offering than Christ, who is perfect God and perfect man, so the Mass should be the primary place where we pray for virtue. Christ also perfectly models the virtues for us (more on this in the next chapter).

Second, in Baptism, we are cleansed of original sin (and any other sins we have committed up to that point in life), brought into the state of grace, die to the life of sin, and are resurrected in Christ. Since the sacrament of Baptism restores us to the state of grace, it is the source of all our infused and theological virtues. Therefore, it is important that we evangelize and bring others to baptism, so that they may have charity, too. This is also why it is important to remember our baptism. St. Peter admonishes us that whoever lacks the virtues has forgotten his baptism (see 2 Peter 1:3-9) because to lack the infused virtues is to lack the state of grace by returning to the life of sin (more on this shortly).

Third, if we do find that we are lacking the virtues, perhaps it is because we have strayed from the faith. Sin has a way of darkening our reasoning so that we do not think that our vices are so bad, or so that we think of virtue as being extreme and unreasonable (see chapter two). In fact, we come to love our sins and fear letting go of them. Thankfully, Christ instituted the sacrament of Reconciliation so that we can confess our sins, be forgiven, and start again with a clean slate.

While we must confess all mortal sins that we are aware of in order to return to the state of grace, it is also a good practice to confess our venial sins in order to weed them out before they lead us into mortal sins. This is the virtue of *penitence*.

If we practice this virtue, we will never stray far from the Faith. Jesus teaches us to forgive others seventy times seven times (see Matthew 18:22), and he is infinitely more merciful than we are. Thus, there is no excuse not to keep trying, to keep asking for forgiveness and getting the boost of grace we need to persevere and grow. The only true obstacle in the way is ourselves, whether it be our fear or our laziness, so we must keep in mind that God rejoices more over a repentant sinner than a righteous person who needs no repentance (see Luke 15:7) and that perfect love, which is offered to us through confession, casts out all fear (see 1 John 4:18).

Finally, if we are in the state of grace, we can partake of the heavenly food for our earthly pilgrimage: the Eucharist. The Eucharist is the true body, blood, soul, and divinity of Christ under the appearance of bread and wine. This food, once consumed, does not become part of us like ordinary food, but instead makes us part of Christ. It elevates us and fills us with charity, since Charity himself comes to dwell within us. The Church teaches that the Eucharist is the "source and summit" of the Christian life:[10] it is the source of unity in the Church since it keeps us in communion with all the members of Christ's mystical body (see 1 Corinthians 10:17), and it gives us a foretaste of the union we will have with God in heaven.[11] The Eucharist, then, is an essential conduit for the increase in the virtues in us. All we need to do is to try our hardest to open ourselves to receive all that is offered in the Eucharist, and to pray for greater openness (before we get distracted by our distracted children or our grumbling stomach).

Clearly prayer—personal prayer and the sacraments—is the most powerful tool we have for growing in virtue. But why is it so powerful? How can God answer our prayer for virtue at all? To understand this, we turn to the relationship between God's and our activity.

Cooperative Action

My family and I were at a small water park one hot summer afternoon. At one point, my son and I were waiting for the others and happened to be standing next to an arcade machine that involved using an electronic device to "hit" targets. My son, who was only four years old at the time, wanted to give it a try.

I watched as he stretched to pick up the device, only for the tip to immediately drop to the ground due to its weight. I stood there for a few seconds, amusedly watching my son spin in circles trying to lift it, before I picked it up for him. I told him that I would aim at the targets and he could push the button. Much to my surprise, my son had good intuition on when to push the button, and by the end of the time limit we had a high score. When it was time to put in our name in the High Score List, we were faced with the question: Whose high score was it? Whose name should go on the list?

Of course, that was not a real-life question. No matter what, I would have put my son's name on the list. But philosophically, it is an interesting question. Who should be praised for the high score? Without my aiming, my son never would have hit a single target. But if he had not been pushing the button, I would have just been waving a device at a monitor—looking quite silly—and earning the same score of zero.

You may be thinking that it is obvious that the score was both of ours, that it was a cooperative effort, and I would agree that it was. But strangely, we often do not view cooperative achievements as cooperative. We award the gymnast with a gold medal for her performance, but not her coach who trained her. While it is true that she would not have won the gold without her performance, it is also true that she would not have won it without her coach's advice. We celebrate the soccer player who scores the winning goal, but not the player who gave him the crucial assist. While we may mark the assist, it does not receive the same credit as the goal scored. But the goal would not have been possible without the pass at the right time.

One might object that these actions are not quite the same as the high score. After all, the training came before the performance, and the pass came before the goal, but the high score was a simultaneous act. This is true. But, then, why do we still have a tendency to separate the responsibility for acts that are even more simultaneous and more united than my and my son's high score? Here I am talking about the actions that we perform in union with God's grace as a result of the virtues infused within us.

Steeped in the Spirit

This word "infused" is not used very commonly today. In my experience, most people only use the word in relation to tea that has been infused with herbs or some other flavor. In this context, infusion refers to the way in which God "pours" grace into our being so that we can act in union with his inspirations. Here, the first definition of "infuse" from the *Cambridge Dictionary* is instructive—"to fill someone or something with an emotion or quality." The virtues are qualities (character traits) of the human soul, and thus an infused virtue is a quality of our character that we receive from God's grace.

As Christians, we acknowledge that we cannot do everything on our own. This is both because of the limits of our finite, created nature and because of the wound of original sin. There are some actions that we need God's help for, such as understanding any aspect of the Trinitarian nature of God or being able to love our neighbor sacrificially out of charity. However, we do not want to go so far in emphasizing God's activity in us that it erases our own individuality and agency. When we speak of God infusing virtues, we should not imagine something akin to Zeus up in the clouds hurling down a lightning bolt at a person, zapping her and possessing her, and then acting through her as if she were a robot.

Perhaps the tea analogy is helpful after all. When tea is infused, we drink the tea and the infused flavor as one; we do not separate the tea and the flavor in our minds when we consider whether we like the beverage. Similarly, in our actions through virtues that have been infused in us, we are not able to separate our action from God's grace and activity; it is a single act involving our cooperation and participation in God's movement.

What Grace Is Not

By this point we have used the word "grace" quite a bit. It is a common word in our culture, and more so when used in a religious context. But what exactly does it mean? As with all things that come from God, grace is mysterious, and so it is helpful to first rule out what grace is not before asserting anything about what it is.

First, in this context, we do not mean "grace" in the same sense in which we say "she dances with grace," or "he lost with grace." Here, grace means something like effortlessness, beauty, or being composed. We also do not mean it in the sense of being gracious or saying grace before a meal, although these get closer to the meaning. This use of grace or gracious refers to thankfulness. To say that someone "fell from grace" gets even closer to our meaning, especially since this expression derives from the Fall of Adam and Eve, even if it can have a secular meaning of falling out of favor with someone. In this expression, grace refers to some state of good favor.

Second, grace does not have quantity in the mathematical sense, although we can speak of gaining or losing grace, increasing in or decreasing in grace. It would be helpful if the Church could create a "Grace-o-meter" that you put on your forehead to calculate how much grace you possess, or whether you are in the state of grace or the state of mortal sin, but this simply is not possible. Grace cannot be measured like weight, size, and temperature because it is not something that can be physically sensed. As a spiritual gift, it cannot be observed under a microscope or measured in any quantitative way.

Instead, it is better to understand grace as a quality (rather than a quantity) of our being, and that we increase in grace when we participate more in it and decrease in grace when we participate less in it. This is similar to how our virtues increase, as explained in chapter one. Our virtues increase when we participate more in the right reason of the mean that pertains to them, but we could never quantify how strong or weak our virtues are.

Another image that we want to avoid is that grace is a part of God. Grace certainly comes from God, and we can describe grace as divine life in us, but it is not a piece of God that we receive. Although we do not have the space here to consider a metaphysics of God, it suffices to say that the Church teaches on sound logical and philosophical grounds that God is absolutely one and simple (that is, not made up of parts), even while being three Persons.

The early councils of the Church condemned various Trinitarian heresies that suggested that God has multiple parts or that one divine Person possesses attributes that the other divine Persons do not. So, grace should not be understood in a pantheistic way, where we receive part of God or even become part of God.[12]

What Grace Is

With these misconceptions out of the way, we can now explain what grace is. The *Catechism of the Catholic Church* defines grace as "the free and undeserved help that God gives us to respond to his call to become children of God, adoptive sons, partakers of the divine nature and of eternal life" (CCC 1996; drawing on John 1:12-18, 17:3; Romans 8:14-17; and 2 Peter 1:3-4). What does this mean? What does becoming a child of God have to do with praying for virtue? As we will soon see—everything!

Grace is free and undeserved. God offers us grace freely, meaning that he is under no obligation to give us grace. Just as much as God was not bound to create anything and creation added nothing to his perfection, so also was God not bound to give us grace and save us from sin. All of this added nothing to his perfection. God is unchanging and perfect, and if he needed to create or give us grace then he would require us for him to be perfect—which would mean that he is imperfect. Nevertheless, although he did not need to do it, God still chose to create and to bestow grace on us out of his merciful love.

Not only does God offer grace gratuitously (i.e., freely), but it is also free for us in the sense that we do not need to earn it. In fact, it is impossible for us to earn it. There is no action that we, as finite, sinful creatures, could perform on our own that would earn any reward from the infinitely good God. However, since Jesus Christ is both God and man, he can earn merit in his humanity. And, since we are all incorporated into Christ through Baptism, we can both receive the rewards for Christ's merits and earn merit through Christ. As explained above, this is through our cooperative actions with God.

In the early centuries of the Church, a prominent heresy was Pelagianism, which held that original sin of our first parents was only a bad example and that it did not result in a weakened human nature that is passed on through birth. Thus, they also believed that humans did not need grace and that we could earn heaven. While we might be tempted to see such claims are obviously false, many Christians have a tendency to approach the moral life with a Pelagian mindset. How often do we think that we need to earn God's help, or that we need to attain a certain degree of virtue on our own before we ask for God's help?

This chapter's strategy reminds us not to wait to pray for God's help; if we do, we may never reach the point where we feel comfortable in praying for it. Grace is help that God gives us, and the Church teaches that we require God's grace to begin, assist, and complete any good act. This is not to say that we have no agency and God does all the work for us. Rather, it is to say that we are deeply wounded by sin and that even what is still good in us needs his help to remain good.

The Power to Be Saints

Think of being in the state of grace as like being plugged in to an electrical outlet. As long as we are plugged in, our batteries are fully charged, and we are able to fulfill our nature. Committing a mortal sin is like getting unplugged. Any good that we do in that state is a result of the charge left from God's grace from creation or our former state of grace (or brief charges he gives us along the way), but the battery is draining fast. In both cases, the good that we do is from our personal acts but achieved in cooperation with God's grace.

Grace helps us to respond to his call to become children of God, adoptive sons, partakers of the divine nature and of eternal life. To say that we are called by God is to say that we have a vocation (literally "calling"), and to say that this call is to become children of God is to say that we all have a fundamental vocation to become holy. Remember, a saint is simply someone who is holy, and everyone in heaven is holy. Thus, we are all called to become saints, and besides that nothing in this world matters.

Being "children of God," "adoptive sons in the Son," and "partakers of the divine nature and of eternal life" are different biblical expressions that mean the same thing. Grace is some participation in divine life.

In the fourth century, St. Athanasius boldly proclaimed that God became man so that man may become like God. This sentiment has been echoed throughout the entire Christian tradition up to the present day. Of course, this is not to be understood in a pantheistic way—we do not lose our individual identity and get absorbed into God. Materially, we always remain distinct from God since he has no parts and has no body (except for the incarnate flesh of the Son).

However, by grace we do become formally like God—that is, we unite our minds and wills to God's mind and will. This is not to be conceived as some strange sort of hive mind, but more akin to how spouses remain separate individuals but can think on the same page and finish each other's sentences. Far from losing our identity by grace, as we have seen, "Christ ... fully reveals man to man himself."[13]

Since God made us for him, it is in uniting with him that we find and become our true selves. Thus, sin and anything that pulls us away from God distorts our true selves and causes us to lose our true identity. Grace repairs this and elevates us. Heaven, though it seems now like a dream, is more real than this world since it consists in union with God, who is life itself. In heaven, then, we will have greater life than we have ever known, and it is this world that will seem like a dream.

State of Grace

While we may never fully understand what grace is, God has revealed to us enough of the mystery that at least we have a foundational understanding. From his revelation we also know that anyone is in the state of grace who has been baptized and has been forgiven of any mortal sins committed since baptism.

It is this state of grace that is like the analogy of being plugged into the outlet, and it is only while in the state of grace that we can consistently think and will in union with God. In other words, it is only in the state of grace that we can consistently cooperate with God in our actions. Recall from the first chapter that a virtue is a habitual and consistent character trait. Without this consistency, we do not have a virtue, but only a disposition. Thus, if we can only consistently cooperate with God in the state of grace, then it is only in the state of grace that we can possess infused virtues.

While scholars debate over the relationship between infused virtues and the natural virtues that we can develop outside of the state of grace, there are some things that are clear. First, it is a fundamental principle of theology that grace perfects nature and does not destroy it. Thus, when we receive infused virtues, they do not destroy or remove any virtues that we may have attained before that point. Again, we do not lose our identity in grace but gain it. God never harms us, but always helps us. Grace simply takes what habits we have already cultivated and elevates them so that we can direct all our activity toward love of God and neighbor, and the attainment of heaven.

Second, although God gives us these virtues by grace, this does not make them any less our own. As we saw earlier in this chapter, God does not possess us or remove our freedom, but instead enlarges our freedom. When we act with faith, hope, charity, or any other infused virtue, we are acting in cooperation with God, but our actions are truly our own. Likewise, infused virtues themselves are true descriptions of our character even though they are given by God. Perhaps a good analogy here is how parents give their children what is their own.

I have given my children their bedrooms, although those rooms still belong to me. The fact that I bought the house and pay the mortgage does not make those bedrooms any less theirs. In time, my children will be able to make their rooms more their own, decorating them and arranging them in ways that are more suitable, which they will then be excited to show me. Just so, God gives us grace and we act on it, producing good works that we offer back to him in thanksgiving. While my children's bedrooms are both mine and theirs, grace is both God's and mine. My children have true freedom in using their bedrooms, as I have true freedom in cooperating with God's grace. It would upset me if my children rejected or trashed their bedrooms, as it would offend God to reject or act against his grace. But even if they did reject their bedrooms, I would continue to offer them a room to sleep, like how God continues to offer us grace even when we reject it.

Grace and Virtues

So the virtues that God gives us by grace build us up and are truly our own. In addition—and this is the most exciting aspect of infused virtue—anyone who is in the state of grace possesses infused virtue. It is not the case that we must first attain the state of grace and then afterwards ask God for infused virtue. Since anyone in the state of grace is sanctified by God, anyone in the state of grace receives the character traits and the help they need to act virtuously. This means that as long as we remain in the state of grace, we are virtuous, and the only way to lose infused virtue is to commit mortal sin and lose the state of grace altogether.

This is quite a comforting conclusion, especially given the discussion of the connection of the virtues in chapter four. We saw there that to possess any virtue we must possess them all, and to possess a single virtue we must have right knowledge, right choice, right action, and enjoyment of the act. There is a lot necessary for a virtue, and without God's constant help it seems nearly impossible. With God, however, all things are possible.

You may be wondering, though, how it is not just a sleight of hand to claim that everyone in the state of grace is virtuous. After all, it does not take much to imagine an example of someone in the state of grace who does not enjoy performing the good. For example, an alcoholic who receives confession is now in the state of grace, but his desire for alcohol does not necessarily vanish as he leaves the confessional. At best, it seems that he can only be continent when it comes to drinking moderately because enjoyment of the good, one of the elements of a virtue, seems to be lacking.

Thomas Aquinas is realistic when it comes to the experience of virtue. He admits that someone in the state of grace may still experience unreasonable desires and not enjoy doing the good, but he asserts that this person still possesses virtue. How can this be?

The reason is that a virtue is a perfection of a human capacity, but there is more than one way for something to be perfect. In one way, a thing can be perfect by lacking nothing. In another way, a thing can be perfect by having the highest excellence. For example, a young piano student may be able to play every scale perfectly, in the sense that he never misses a correct note. He plays perfectly insofar as he made no mistakes. A more advanced student may play a composition of Mozart, making a couple of mistakes in the midst of it. The advanced student would not have the perfection of completion that the novice student has, since the advanced student missed a few notes. But clearly playing Mozart is a more perfect use of a piano than playing a C scale. Playing Mozart is a greater perfection because scales are not meant to be played for their own sake but rather to become the backbone of beautiful music. The advanced student possesses this second perfection, even if he does not yet possess the first perfection in his playing of Mozart.

The virtues that we acquire apart from the state of grace have the first type of perfection, where nothing is lacking. They entail right reason, choice, action, and enjoyment. Infused virtues have the second type of perfection, insofar as grace directs our acts not to some natural or worldly good but to the supernatural good of our union with God. While the acts that flow from acquired virtues are truly good, acts of infused virtues are even better because they are done for love of God and neighbor and merit eternal salvation for us. Even if they are done without enjoyment, and thus they lack the first type of perfection, they are still more excellent than acts of acquired virtues. Why? Because they lead to supernatural and everlasting happiness. In time, with the help of grace, our infused virtues may grow and attain the first type of perfection. In the meantime, we are still virtuous.

It is worth noting here that even when we attain both types of perfection in virtue, there will always be room to grow. We can always get closer and closer to the virtuous mean. We can continue to grow in deeper understanding and greater enjoyment of what is good. We will never reach the upper limit of a virtue, whether a natural virtue or an infused virtue. Even the virtuous person has room to grow.

Theological Virtues

The key to acting for our supernatural end, as just mentioned, is that we act with love of God and neighbor. In other words, we act out of charity.

Charity (sometimes simply called "love") is one of the three theological virtues along with *faith* and *hope*. These three virtues are a special subset of virtues for two reasons: 1) they are virtues that we can only possess by grace. We can never acquire them by our own efforts, and 2) they are specifically perfections of our relationship with God, rather than perfections of our responses to things in this world. In contrast, infused prudence, infused justice, infused courage, and infused temperance are oriented toward how we act regarding ourselves and our neighbors, even though we possess these virtues by grace. The theological virtues are oriented directly toward God. Since these virtues deal directly with our relationship with God and this chapter's strategy is to turn to God in prayer, understanding what these theological virtues are will help us all the more with this strategy. The greater our faith, hope, and charity, the greater ease and motivation we will have in living out the cardinal virtues.

Faith, as an intellectual virtue, provides us with a new worldview that includes God and all that he has revealed. Thus, faith gives us new eyes for seeing the world. For example, we no longer see the cashier at the grocery store as just a stranger or the annoying coworker as just an irritation, but we see each person as a child of God for whom Christ died. Our eating and exercise habits are no longer just to prolong our life but now also to respect the temple of the Holy Spirit that is our body.

Faith is the virtue that allows us to firmly believe in God as truth itself and in all that God has revealed, such as the things we recite in the creed at Mass. Although it is belief in things unseen, it is nevertheless more certain than even the knowledge of things we acquire in the world. It is firm because all that is revealed comes directly from the source of truth itself—God.

Hope can often be a confusing virtue because "hope" is also the name of an emotion we experience. When we experience hope as an emotion, we strongly desire some good thing that is difficult to obtain and not yet present to us, yet still possible. Sometimes, it is akin to wishful thinking: "I hope I get a good grade on the exam," or "I hope I get a big bonus this year." We hope because the outcome is uncertain.

The theological virtue of hope, however, is most certain. The virtue of hope is better described as the habit of seeking God as the source of our ultimate happiness, of pursuing God because of all of the good things he has promised us (such as resurrection from death, everlasting life, and a glorified body). God's promises to us are certain because he never breaks his promises. If he says that we can inherit life everlasting by believing in his Son, getting baptized, repenting of our sins, and partaking of the Eucharist, then we can hope with absolute certainty that we will receive that reward for fulfilling those requirements.

What we cannot know with absolute certainty, however, is whether we will fulfill those requirements. Therefore, we always depend on God's grace and why we need to pray for his assistance. The virtue of hope ensures that we do maintain a consistent prayer life so that we can attain the things God has promised us. Hope, therefore, is the virtuous mean between the vices of despair and presumption. Despair is the vice of not believing that God will deliver on his promises (especially for me), while presumption is the vice of believing that I can attain the rewards God promises without having to fulfill the requirements he sets.

Charity

The final theological virtue is the greatest of them all because it shapes all our other virtues and because it is the only theological virtue that we continue to possess in heaven. Faith will pass away and become knowledge of God, and hope will pass away and become enjoyment of our rewards. But the third theological virtue will endure—the virtue of charity.

Unfortunately, the names that we have for this virtue narrow our understanding of it. The traditional name for the virtue is charity, deriving from the Latin *caritas*. Today, when we hear "charity" we think of donating money to the poor or to a cause. That is one example of an act of charity among thousands. The other name, "love," does not do justice to the virtue either because it leads us to think of love in human terms. In the English language, we have one word for love, and it is the same word whether we are talking about love of God, love of my spouse, love of my country, love of my children, love of my job, love of my pet, love of football, or love of pizza. Hopefully we do not have the same type of love for all these things! Other languages, such as Greek and Latin, have a wide array of terms referring to each type of love: *amor, dilectio, storge, philia, eros, venus, caritas.*

When we speak of charity, we are not referring to a human love. We are instead referring to the love with which God loves himself. Take a moment to reread that sentence and let it sink in. Charity is the love with which God loves himself. It is the love that the Father gives eternally to the Son, the love that the Son eternally receives from the Father, and the love that the Son eternally gives back to the Father. And God is that very love. As we read in 1 John 4:16, "God is love," and the term used is *caritas* (or *agape* in the original Greek).

A little exercise in logic reveals something profound: If God is charity, and we are not God, then we are not charity. Thus, we cannot possess charity apart from God; it is something we can only possess by grace. But when we are given charity by grace, that means that we are given a habit of character that enables us to love God and neighbor with the very love with which God loves himself. This is extraordinary!

When the *Catechism* speaks of partaking of the divine nature, or when St. Athanasius says that God will make us like him, they are referring to charity. Charity is the virtue that unites us with God, the virtue which allows us to unite our will to his and to think in union with his wisdom. Charity conforms us to Christ, because Christ is the human incarnation of the love of God. God is love, and Christ is God, so Christ is love. And if we are baptized into Christ and become members of his mystical body, then we are conformed to charity, that is, to the very love of God. Put more simply: we are conformed to God.

Pope Benedict XVI in his third encyclical stated that "charity is love received and given."[14] On the human level, this means that we must first receive charity from God before we can give it back to God and neighbor. And we do not truly possess charity if we jealously hold on to it and fail to give it to others. This is because, on the divine level, the charity that God is consists of three divine Persons who eternally receive the other two Persons and give themselves back to the other two Persons. The three Persons of the Trinity are one God and they share everything with each other. The only thing that distinguishes them are the relations between them regarding how they each give and receive that one shared love. Since we are made in the image of the Trinity, we are called to receive and live out the same unconditional and sacrificial love.

Every Prayer Is Answered

The essence of charity is something that we could ponder for the rest of our lives and never fully plumb its depths. In fact, if we get to heaven, we will ponder and experience it for life everlasting and still will not fully plumb its depths. It is something we should always return to contemplate, because if we believe in charity then we have every reason to constantly rejoice. It is the most incredible gift.

But we may feel that our charity is low, that our love is weak. Likewise, we are aware of our vices and the other virtues that we struggle to live out. If God loves us so much, why does he not make us perfect now? While none of us can speak for the divine mind, we can all acknowledge that we have responsibility if we are to attain these virtues. Thus, it falls on us to try our hardest, but more importantly to always pray for God's help. Pray for virtue, pray for perseverance in striving for virtue ... even pray for the desire to strive for virtue! Prayer and the sacraments, then, are not a last resort but a first resort, and a resort at every turn.

We should never strive for virtue apart from prayer, and we will find much greater success if we have ample recourse to prayer. Still, we must recognize that our increase in virtue will occur in God's timing rather than ours, so we should not be discouraged if it takes great time and effort. The truth is, we will never reach the peak of virtue in this life, and so will always be able to improve. This, however, should be cause for excitement rather than discouragement, because we have our whole lives to draw closer to God and become more ourselves.

Strategies

1. Fake it till you make it.

2. Overshoot the target.

3. Breaking the habit.

4. Know thyself.

5. A friend in need is a friend indeed.

6. **Let go and let God** — Begin praying for virtue and take advantage of the graces available in the sacraments.

7

Do As I Say and As I Do

End-of-life care is a very emotional time, not only for those who are dying but also for their family members. In my own experience, as family members have passed away, every scenario has been different. Some passed away abruptly, others very slowly. In every case, we never want to watch someone suffer, and we try to do what is best for our loved ones.

There is a particular suffering for those who take care of their loved ones, especially if they must make medical decisions for them. Often those who have been entrusted with such decisions ask, what do we do? What is the moral choice here? Am I a bad person for making this choice?

The particular challenge with these questions is that there generally are not clear answers to them. While there are some clear parameters, such as that you cannot euthanize a person or deprive them of basic care, for the most part the moral evaluation of what is right and wrong depends on the particular situation. Do we attempt the experimental drug that may possibly extend life for a few weeks but is very costly? Do we transfer our loved one to home hospice care where he will be around family but may pass away slightly sooner? It is in times like these that we ask, what are the rules? Someone tell me what I have to do!

Just because there may not be one-size-fits-all rules to apply across these diverse situations does not mean that there is not objective truth about what is right or wrong. However, it takes more effort than usual to figure this out. What is necessary in these moments is true prudence. Often, it comes down to forming our conscience as best as we can with the data and expert opinions that we have at hand and going with our decision. We try our best and leave it in God's hands.

Occasionally, the Catholic understanding of virtue gets criticized because it is difficult to live and is not black and white. Many see a system of ethics based on simple rules as much more comfortable and clear—just follow the rules to be good, and I am free wherever there are no rules.

Yet just because something is difficult does not mean it is not worth doing. In fact, most things worth doing are difficult. Think of keeping a happy marriage, raising children, getting an education, caring for sick relatives, etc.

Rules

Contrary to what some may think, there is a lot of "black and white" in virtue ethics. In chapter five, we discussed intrinsic evils that may never be chosen, whereas in chapter two we presented vices we must avoid—and saw that all the virtues spring from the foundation of the Ten Commandments. However, determining the virtuous choice in a given situation can be difficult. As we have all probably experienced, there is some variation and subjectivity within the objective bounds of right and wrong. As referenced above, while it would be objectively immoral to kill a suffering patient, it will depend on the patient whether risky or experimental surgeries should be attempted, when palliative care should be used, how much pain medication to administer, or whether to forego certain interventions and to allow a natural death. While bioethics has certain principles to follow in answering these questions, the application of these principles will depend on the specific circumstances. In other words, prudence is required.

This should not be seen as a weakness of the Catholic understanding of virtue, but rather as a strength. Virtue theory takes seriously the complexities of life and can give general guidance in areas where rules and laws do not reach. Furthermore, the practice of virtue allows us to truly flourish as humans and to act dynamically. If we restricted ourselves just to rules, we could follow them all and still be miserable people. For example, a person could follow all the Commandments—never murdering anyone, never committing adultery, never missing Mass, never stealing, and never lying—but still be a total jerk and burdensome to be around.

Rules are not the fullness of morality, but the starting point. We cannot be virtuous without following the basic moral rules, but in time we internalize these rules and do not see them as restrictions of our freedom, but rather the cause of our freedom. Take an example: When we are young, our parents have to teach us not to eat glass, not to drink the fun-colored liquids under the sink, and not to stick small things up our nose. But when we get older, nobody thinks, "Man, I really wish I could eat glass! It would be so much fun to stick a watch battery up my nose!" We recognize how bad and painful these actions would be for our health, and we internalize these bodily norms to the point where we do not even see them as rules limiting our freedom. Instead, they are the obvious basis for living a healthy life—so healthy, in fact, that they do not even need to be stated.

The moral life should be similar. The Ten Commandments should be so obvious to us that they do not even need to be stated. The fact that we do need to state them shows our moral immaturity. But as we grow in moral maturity, we internalize them and do not see them as rules limiting our freedom but instead as the foundation for our true happiness. And just as we would not say avoiding eating glass is the peak of bodily health, neither is avoiding murdering a person the peak of moral perfection. There is a great expanse beyond the rules, and this is the domain of virtue.

Still, as this book and our life experience show, growth in virtue is difficult. How do we figure out how to act virtuously in those areas not defined by rules? The final strategy of this book is to *find and imitate a virtuous person*. These people have gone before us and done a lot of the hard work in determining what works and what does not. We are free to choose to go it alone and repeat all their mistakes, or we can take their advice, imitate them, and make progress a little faster.

Finding the Wise Person

The strategy of finding a virtuous person to imitate dates at least as far back as Aristotle. It was Aristotle's conviction that only a person late in life can acquire prudence, since prudence requires the ability to make good judgments in diverse scenarios and to do this requires much experience.

We are all familiar with the "wise man" trope from fantasy stories (wizards with long, gray beards) and east-Asian cultures (again, portrayed with long, gray beards). We also have a cultural sense that our grandparents can share great wisdom and should be sought for advice. Of course, being old does not automatically make one wise and prudent, especially if the person lived a vicious life. However, it is more likely that an older person will have acquired practical wisdom than a young person. After all, young people so often act on impulse and have little life experience.

So, a good starting point in seeking out the virtuous person to imitate may be our elders. By asking them questions about how they handled situations and heeding their advice, we may find insight into how to make our own virtuous decisions.

They are not the only models of virtue, however. We know that working on any virtue helps with all of them (see chapter four). It is possible that we may find great examples of temperance, fortitude, justice, or any of their sub-virtues in younger people.

But perhaps we do not know anybody personally with great virtue, or at least not anyone who is consistently virtuous and worthy of imitation. Perhaps we turn to heroes in sports or celebrities, only to later find them exposed for some great scandal. If this is our situation, we do not need to despair. The Church has identified for us thousands of examples of people who, despite making many (and sometimes grievous) mistakes along the way, ended their lives and sometimes lived their entire lives with heroic virtue. These are the saints.

There are enough canonized saints that everyone can find at least one whom he can relate to. By reading about the lives of the saints and praying through their intercession, we enter into the school of virtue with the saint as our teacher.

Heavenly Intercession

While we often talk about praying to the saints, learning about their lives, and imitating them, they can feel so distant from us and removed from our earthly experience. The truth is that their life in heaven allows them to be closer to us than if they were on earth, and they are all aware of us even if we are not aware of them. An old acquaintance once told me a story that has always stuck with me and really brought to life for me the closeness of the saints. He told me about the unique experience of a seminarian friend he had—we will call him Jim—on the weekend of his ordination to the priesthood.

As the story goes, Jim had a strong devotion to St. Sebastian, an early Christian martyr. At the rehearsal for the ordination, the seminarians were told that any saint they requested would be added to the litany of the saints that is recited during the ordination. Naturally, Jim requested St. Sebastian. At the end of the rehearsal, the coordinator reminded the seminarians that if they thought of any other saints that they wanted added to the litany, they could send a quick email in the morning.

That night, Jim awoke from his sleep feeling strongly that St. Philip Neri had to be added to the litany. He was aware of St. Philip, an Italian priest of the sixteenth century known both for his incredible devotion to the Eucharist and his sense of humor, but he had no particular devotion to him. Still, it weighed heavily on his heart that St. Philip needed to be added to the litany, so he sent a quick email. The thought had come so suddenly and strongly out of the blue that he figured there must be a reason for it.

At the ordination, Jim listened attentively as the litany was chanted. One by one, the names went by, until St. Philip Neri was sung. "Oh, good! They got my email," he thought. But where was St. Sebastian? The names continued on and on, and then the litany was over. No Sebastian. Jim was a bit disappointed, but he was glad that Philip Neri got in for whatever strange reason he felt compelled to request him.

Soon after, with this incident fresh in his mind, Jim got an opportunity to meet a holy priest with charismatic gifts who offered to pray over him, stating whatever came to him by inspiration. The priest began to pray and paused. There was a quizzical look on his face. After a brief silence, he said, "I see St. Philip Neri ... he's laughing at you."

Fr. Jim's jaw dropped to the floor. Only he understood what was going on. The priest had not attended the ordination Mass, had never met Fr. Jim, and knew nothing about his requests for the litany. As Fr. Jim tells the story, he was pranked by St. Philip Neri from heaven! Ever since then, while he has not stopped praying through the intercession of St. Sebastian, he now has a deep devotion to Philip as well.

The point is that the saints are close to us, whether we realize it or not. They are already actively interceding for us even before we even pray for their intercession. All the more can we benefit from direct contact with them through prayer and the imitation of their lives. Just as we seek the wisdom of the elderly for their life experience, all the more should we seek the wisdom of the saintly for their experience of having succeeded and, in the words of St. Paul, "finished the race" (2 Timothy 4:7).

Understanding Conscience

By this point in the book, it should be clear that imitating any virtue will help growth in all the virtues. However, we have also seen how prudence has a somewhat elevated role since without prudence we would not be able to identify just, courageous, and temperate acts. Thus, while imitating any virtue is helpful, we want to make sure that we are also trying to imitate prudence. While this can be done through seeking the wisdom of elders or the saints, another simple way to do this is through studying morality. Here is another way to tap into the experience of the wise.

For example, by reading this book you have already taken in some of the wisdom of Aristotle, St. Paul, St. Thomas Aquinas, and Jesus himself. Whether it be a moral treatise by a saint or Catholic theologian, or a document from the pope or another bishop, studying these texts is studying the inherited wisdom of a two-thousand-year tradition. Among these texts, pride of place should be given to the New Testament and the *Catechism of the Catholic Church.* The American bishops even released a *Compendium of the Catechism of the Catholic Church* which summarizes the *Catechism* into a fraction of its length. Once we have read these texts and learned from them, we can put them into practice.

More than merely suggesting that we study morality, the Church teaches that we have a moral duty to do so. This is because our understanding of morality shapes our judgments of conscience, which in turn enables us to act prudently. The Church teaches two principles regarding conscience. To prepare ourselves to take in the wisdom we find as we study, let us first clarify what conscience is, and then explain each principle in turn.

It may sound a bit pedantic to say that we need to explain what conscience is, but its true meaning has been quite obscured through media. The way that conscience is presented in media today is through a "shoulder angel" and a "shoulder devil." I am sure we are all familiar with at least one show or cartoon that displays this trope, whether it be *Looney Tunes, Full House,* or *The Emperor's New Groove.* The angel is always dressed in white and encouraging the character to do what is right, while the devil is dressed in red or seductively and tempts the character to choose what is evil. Often the angel is depicted as boring and the devil as exciting. The angel and demon depict the interior monologue of the main character trying to decide what to do. The problem with this depiction is that conscience is presented as two conflicting voices that do not actually help the character to decide. Even if we claim instead that these images are really depicting two separate voices of temptation and conscience, conscience is still presented as more of a suggestion or plea rather than a firm judgment.

A closer depiction to the true meaning of conscience can be found in Disney's *Pinocchio.* In this movie, Jiminy Cricket is made the conscience of Pinocchio by his fairy godmother. The fairy tells Jiminy that he is to be to Pinocchio a "still, small voice," the "keeper of the knowledge of right and wrong," a "counselor in moments of temptation," and a "guide along the straight and narrow path." Rather than suggesting what Pinocchio should do, Jiminy Cricket assertively tells him. Pinocchio may still act against his conscience, but this is also realistic.

The *Catechism of the Catholic Church* defines conscience as "a judgment of reason whereby the human person recognizes the moral quality of a concrete act that he is going to perform, is in the process of performing, or has already completed" (CCC 1778). In other words, conscience is a moral judgment about an action that was, is, or will be performed. It is what we truly believe in our heart of hearts is right.

Judging versus Judgmentalism

Note that conscience is a judgment. As we have seen, we are always making judgments in the moral life. It is unavoidable. For us to choose any moral object at all, we must judge that it is in some way good for us. We choose it over other objects that we judge to be less good, or even bad, for us. So, when we hear people say that this or that person "has no conscience," strictly speaking this is incorrect. It is impossible for anyone to not have a conscience because it is impossible that any free moral agent not make moral judgments. What we mean by the expression is that the person makes an incorrect judgment of conscience, and therefore chooses what is evil.

We must be careful to note that making moral judgments is not the same as being judgmental. We can remember passages in the Gospel where Jesus warns us not to judge others, such as "Judge not, that you be not judged. For with the judgment you pronounce you will be judged, and the measure you give will be the measure you get" (Matthew 7:1-2). However, we also find passages where Jesus specifically instructs us to reprove someone who has sinned, and sometimes to do so publicly: "If your brother sins against you, go and tell him his fault, between you and him alone ... [I]f he does not listen, take one or two others along with you, that every word may be confirmed by the evidence of two or three witnesses. If he refuses to listen to them, tell it to the church" (Matthew 18:15-17). How are we to reconcile these passages?

St. Thomas Aquinas reminds us that judging is a normal intellectual activity that we must perform for any truly voluntary action. For me to choose this rather than that, I must have made some prior judgment that this is better than that under these circumstances. For example, if I choose to forgive a person who offended me, it is because I have judged that it is better to attempt to mend the relationship than to harbor resentment. If I choose to sleep in and skip work, it is because I have judged that sleeping is better for me than going to work. We cannot avoid judging, because to eliminate judging would necessarily eliminate all free and voluntary action—it would eliminate all virtue and vice! If we eliminate judging, we eliminate human nature, and we become like robots who cannot think or choose for themselves but are pre-programmed for certain actions.

We are constantly judging because everything we choose to do we perceive as good for us, and we want to be happy. The problem is that we often misjudge what is good or what will truly make us happy. The task of ethics, therefore, is to help us to make *correct* judgments.

So, while we can and must make judgments about what is good and evil, what we cannot do—and what Jesus forbids us from doing—is being judgmental toward others, that is, treating others without due respect because of the choices that they make. While we can judge that a particular action of a person was good or evil, we cannot treat him as less than a person made in the image and likeness of God if we determine that he chose something evil. This does not mean that we need to ignore his action; in fact, the quote from Matthew 18 above teaches that we are obliged out of charity to correct those who do wrong (but review the full passage for the correct way to go about doing this). Such correction may even include punishment or cutting ties, but we must remember that even these are sought for the person's correction and not out of a place of hurt or desire for revenge. If we seek the correction of the other, then we are loving him and desiring his salvation; if we seek revenge or belittlement, we are only loving ourselves and desiring his hurt. It is this latter activity that Jesus forbids, because ultimately it makes us evil.

As we imitate the virtuous person, we will observe how they navigate judging acts properly while not becoming judgmental toward others. As we imitate them in this regard, we will be continuously forming our conscience to make better judgments.

Forming One's Conscience

What we have said of conscience so far already leads us to the Church's two principles of conscience. They are that 1) we must always follow our conscience, and 2) we must continuously form our conscience. These are both very important and need to go together.

It may sound strange to say that we should always follow our conscience, especially since we acknowledged that people can make erroneous judgments of conscience. The key to understanding this principle is to recall the discussion of object and intention from chapter five.

When it comes to our conscience, we either make a correct judgment or an erroneous judgment, and we either follow our judgment or not. This gives us four possibilities: 1) follow a correct conscience; 2) reject a correct conscience; 3) follow an erroneous conscience; 4) reject an erroneous conscience.

The first two scenarios are clear-cut. On the one hand, if we make an accurate judgment of conscience and follow it, this means that we accurately judge what is good and do it. Our object and intention are both good. An example would be tithing to the Church in order to help the poor. On the other hand, if we reject a correct conscience, we choose what is evil, knowing that it is evil. Thus, our object and intention are both evil. An example would be gossiping about a coworker in order to ruin her reputation when we know this is an evil act. Thus, the first scenario is a virtuous act while the second scenario is a vicious act.

The third and fourth scenarios are a bit more complex. In both cases, the person misjudges what is right and wrong. As a result, she believes something evil is good or that something good is evil. There could be a whole range of reasons why the person misjudges. Briefly, we can simply state that the person is ignorant of some moral truth, and that ignorance could be outside of the person's control (and therefore remove responsibility for her action), within the person's control (and therefore only somewhat lessen or not lessen at all her responsibility) or be deliberately fostered (and therefore increase her responsibility for her immoral action).

If a person, therefore, follows an incorrect conscience (scenario three), she objectively chooses something immoral but does so with a good intention. Remember that one's judgment of conscience is what she believes in her heart of hearts is the right thing to do. So, even if the person is mistaken about what is good, she still intends to do what is good and chooses what she thinks is good.

While a good intention cannot make an evil object good, it can lessen the evil of the act. Further, the less responsible the person is for her ignorance, the less responsible she is for the immoral act. Following an erring conscience is problematic because the person chooses an immoral object, but at least the evil of the act is lessened somewhat. An example of this scenario might be a Catholic couple choosing to use contraception because they do not have the economic means to raise another child. Their conscience tells them that contraception is a good action. This is incorrect, as the Church teaches contraception is an intrinsic evil. However, their intention is good insofar as they are trying to be responsible and want to prevent raising their children in a state of destitution. A good intention cannot make an evil object good, so their act of contracepting is still an evil act. But the good intention somewhat lessens the evil, and if they act out of ignorance their responsibility may be even further lessened. If they had been wrongly told by a priest that contraception is OK, they may even be invincibly ignorant of the Church's true teaching.

This is not the case in the fourth scenario. In this scenario, a person rejects her incorrect conscience. She chooses what she believes to be immoral, when in fact it is good (since her judgment about it is wrong). Thus, there is a good object and an evil intention, but an evil intention always makes the act evil. While the person may objectively do something good, even something that benefits others, it still damages her own soul since it is done with the intention to do evil. This scenario seems rarer today because many people are moral relativists: if a person thinks everything is permissible, it is much harder to act against that judgment! However, an example might be a person who believes euthanasia is a good thing that should be applied to anyone with chronic suffering (this is an incorrect moral judgment) but chooses not to euthanize her suffering parent because she harbors unforgiveness against her parent and wants him to suffer. Thus, she acts against her conscience. While the person actually does a good thing by not euthanizing her parent, she chooses this because she wills harm to her parent, which is evil.

Thus, taking our four scenarios together, it is always evil and vicious to choose against one's conscience (as in scenarios two and four). Doing so will always harm one's soul because it always involves choosing what the person takes to be evil because he knows it to be evil. However, when someone follows his conscience, he does a virtuous act if his conscience is well-formed, as in scenario one, or at least he may have a decreased responsibility for doing something immoral if his conscience is erroneous and he acts out of ignorance, as in scenario three. This is why the Church teaches that we must always follow our conscience; the alternative is always to willfully choose evil.

	Follow Conscience	Reject Conscience
Correct Conscience	Virtuous	Sinful Vicious
Erroneous Conscience	Mitigated Culpability	Sinful Vicious

However, this also highlights why we are in constant need of forming our consciences well. If we do not form our consciences, we will find ourselves in that third scenario. While our responsibility may be lessened, we are still performing objectively immoral acts, and this will always have some detrimental effect on the soul.

It is also essential for virtue that we form our consciences. Why? Because we cannot have prudence without a well-formed conscience. Prudence is the virtue of identifying the good to be chosen and then choosing it, but if we make mistakes in judging what is good then we will never be able to choose it (or will only do so coincidentally). Thus, without a well-formed conscience, we cannot be prudent, and without prudence we cannot possess the other virtues.

This brings us back to the strategy for this chapter. Through imitating those with prudence or other virtues or taking in their wisdom when we study ethics and read Church teaching on morality, we are forming our consciences. Think of your conscience like a judge in court. A judge cannot make an accurate verdict without evidence. It is by forming our consciences that we can supply evidence to our conscience. Only then can it make accurate judgments.

To extend the analogy further, a judge could convey a guilty sentence but law enforcement may not carry it out. Likewise, it is possible for us to choose against our conscience, but we can never have true virtue if we do so, just as the society could never be just if law enforcement and the courts are not working together.

But do not fear that because we are obliged to form our conscience that we each have to get an advanced degree in moral theology. Aside from studying texts, there are ample opportunities for forming our consciences, including imitating faithful and virtuous Catholics, attending adult faith formation talks at the parish, listening to audio books, reading the lives of the saints, or simply asking your pastor questions.

Jesus Christ as the Wise Man

To conclude this final strategy for growing in virtue, there is one final consideration when it comes to imitating the wise person. Can only the elderly be virtuous? After, all prudence requires experience, and it seems that we need advanced age to have adequate experience. How does this fit into our understanding that anyone in the state of grace possesses virtue? Many people enter the state of grace when they are young—even as infants—and therefore lack the experience necessary for prudence. How, then, can we reconcile these claims?

In the words of the philosopher Angela McKay Knobel,

> Aristotle says that the young lack [prudence] because they lack
> experience, but he also says—importantly—that those who wish to
> become virtuous should find a [prudent person] to imitate. It is the
> availability of a virtuous exemplar, more than any particular set of
> facts about the world, which enables the cultivation of [prudence].
> ... The actions of the exemplar are the guide for the person who
> is learning to exercise [prudence]. When he reaches the point at
> which he can grasp the features of the situation that his exemplar
> grasps, his education is complete.[15]

What Knobel is showing here is that just because experience is necessary for
prudence does not mean that young people cannot be prudent. While a young
person does lack personal experience, he can imitate a prudent person and
so makes the prudent person's experiences his own. In this way, imitation of
virtuous people becomes a sort of shortcut to virtue since it supplies us with
much of the experience we need.

If this can be true on a natural level between people who are removed from
one another, all the more can this occur on a supernatural level. When it comes
to grace and the infused virtues, Jesus Christ is the wise man that we imitate.
When we are in the state of grace, the entire Trinity dwells within us, and we
acknowledge the Holy Spirit as the Person who brings us into contact with
Christ and conforms us to the image of Christ. This is why we are temples of
the Holy Spirit (see 1 Corinthians 6:19).

Thus, when we are in the state of grace and conformed to Christ, God supplies
us with the "experience" that we need in order to imitate Christ. We call
these the gifts of the Holy Spirit: wisdom, understanding, counsel, fortitude,
knowledge, piety, and fear of the Lord. These gifts enable our souls to be open
to the immediate promptings of the Holy Spirit, so that God can more directly
move us (still with our cooperation) to perform perfect acts of imitation of
Christ which exceed even the acts of the virtues. These gifts, therefore, perfect
our virtues, and the good news is that we also possess them as long as we are
in the state of grace.

This leads us back to the central claim of chapter six, and the most important claim of the book. While there are many different strategies for growing in virtue—some that will work better for some people and others that will work better for other people—we will have greater success if we combine some of the strategies. Above all, we must remember to combine any and every strategy with the strategy to pray and receive the sacraments. For "with God all things are possible" (Matthew 19:26).

Strategies

1. Fake it till you make it.

2. Overshoot the target.

3. Breaking the habit.

4. Know thyself.

5. A friend in need is a friend indeed.

6. Let go and let God.

7. **Do as I say, and as I do** — Find and imitate a virtuous person. Read the life of a saint, pray for their intercession, and strive to imitate their virtues. The ultimate virtuous person to imitate is Christ.

Conclusion

We have covered a lot of material and presented many strategies. It may be a nice refresher to review what we have considered.

The strategy explained in the first chapter was the need for repetition of good acts with increasing intensity for the development of virtue. While repeatedly acting well may seem obvious, this strategy is commonly misunderstood to entail mere repetition of an act without any attention to the intensity of the act, which is the true key for developing a stronger virtue. As this strategy is the most fundamental, it is a good starting point for anyone desiring virtue. Setting incremental and achievable goals for acting with greater intensity will work well, along with deepening our understanding of why virtuous actions are truly virtuous. In order to help understand how to act with greater intensity, chapter one explained the most fundamental aspects of virtue: what a virtue is, how a habit (i.e., a virtue or vice) differs from a disposition, and how intensity is more important than quantity in the repetition of our acts.

The second chapter presented the strategy of aiming for the opposite extreme, which we called "overshooting the target." The chapter explained how a virtue is a "mean" or conceptual midpoint between two extreme ways of acting (vices), which are extreme either by acting in a way that is deficient or excessive regarding what is reasonable. As we saw, this strategy works because people tend toward one extreme or the other and misperceive what is virtuous as vicious. It can be helpful to aim for the opposite extreme (i.e., over-compensate) because we will likely fall short of that extreme, landing instead very near the virtuous mean. Our misperceptions actually will self-limit our actions so that we end up doing what is virtuous and, over time, begin to recognize it as truly virtuous. To help us better locate the right targets, we saw what a vice is and also took a brief look at different sets of virtues and their contrary vices.

Whereas the first two strategies involve directly trying to acquire a new virtuous habit, the third strategy entails instead withdrawing from a bad habit. The third chapter helped us to turn inward and reflect on our own tendencies and vices. Presenting the classic four stages of growth in virtue (vice, incontinence, continence, and virtue), chapter three described the distinguishing marks of each stage and what a person needs to focus on in order to move into the next stage. By mapping out where we fall on this four-stage schema, we come to greater self-knowledge, which also benefits us in practicing the fourth strategy.

The strategy in chapter four is to know oneself; to analyze one's strengths and weaknesses and to use those strengths to one's advantage. This chapter revealed the best-kept secret of virtue ethics: how the virtues are connected and how growth in one virtue brings about growth in all virtues. Amazingly, if working on a weak virtue does not bear fruit, working on an already strong virtue can help develop the weaker virtue.

The fifth strategy is to have an accountability partner. People can often be blind to their own shortcomings, whereas these same shortcomings may be obvious to someone else. A trusted accountability partner can help us to discern whether we are truly growing in virtue or instead possess a tricky false virtue or need to straighten out our intentions.

The sixth chapter discussed prayer and the sacraments as one of the surest ways to grow in virtue. Rather than trying to achieve a certain level of perfection before we ask God for help, we can turn to prayer and the sacraments from the very start. It is through grace that Christians receive the theological virtues of faith, hope, and charity, as well as an elevation of the cardinal virtues, and the Christian acting by graced virtues is truly praiseworthy for his actions.

The final strategy is to imitate the virtuous person. Though finding a good role model may seem difficult, fortunately, Jesus Christ is Virtue Incarnate and the model and embodiment of all the virtues. His Holy Spirit comes to dwell within every Christian, revealing the Son of God to us.

The life of virtue is difficult, but it is most worthwhile. Thankfully, we do not have to attempt it blindly or all alone, as these time-tested strategies from the

Catholic tradition give us sure guidance and remind us of how we can be of help to each other, as well as how the whole communion of saints can assist us. Above all, there is no one who desires our virtue and holiness more than God himself.

While the journey may be long and difficult, we must always remember to be patient with ourselves. God wants us to be virtuous even more than we do because he loves us infinitely and wants us to be truly happy—and he is ever patient with us. We can be sure that if we ask for God's help and make our best effort, he will give us the exact help that we need and will see to it that we reach the goal. The only real obstacle in the way is ourselves.

So, it is time that we take our next step, keeping these strategies in mind and praying for the perseverance to never give up. As Jesus, who lived a life of perfect virtue and is the greatest example we should follow, says, "Take my yoke upon you, and learn from me; for I am gentle and lowly in heart, and you will find rest for your souls" (Matthew 11:29).

Notes

1. See Decree on Priestly Formation *Optatam totius*, 16. St. John Paul II makes explicit reference to this document in *Veritatis splendor*, 7, which is a response to Vatican II's call.

2. St. John Paul II, *Veritatis splendor*.

3. Marieke A. Adriaanse, Gabriele Oettingen, Peter M. Gollwitzer, Erin P. Hennes, Denise T. D. de Ridder, John B. F. de Wit, "When planning is not enough: Fighting unhealthy snacking habits by mental contrasting with implementation intentions (MCII)," *European Journal of Social Psychology*, vol. 40, no. 7 (December 2010), 1277–1293.

4. Navin Kaushal and Ryan E. Rhodes, "Exercise Habit Formation in New Gym Members: A Longitudinal Study," *Journal of Behavioral Medicine*, 38 (2015), 652–663.

5. Aristotle, *Nicomachean Ethics*, Book 2, chapter 9; Thomas Aquinas, *Commentary on Aristotle's Nicomachean Ethics*, Book 2, lecture 11.

6. Pope Francis, encyclical letter *Lumen fidei*, 53.

7. Second Vatican Council, *Gaudium et spes*, 22.

8. See Second Vatican Council, *Gaudium et spes*, 24.

9. The dogma of the Immaculate Conception was defined in the encyclical *Ineffabilis Deus*, issued by Pope Pius IX in 1854.

10. Second Vatican Council, *Lumen gentium*, 11.

11. St. Thomas Aquinas, *Summa theologiae*, III, 73, 4.

12. Pantheism is the pagan religious belief that the entire world and everything in it is literally a part of God.

13. Second Vatican Council, *Gaudium et spes*, 22.

14. Benedict XVI, *Caritas in veritate*, 5.

15. Angela Knobel, "Insight, Experience, and the Notion of 'Infused' Virtue," *American Catholic Philosophical Quarterly 90*, 4 (2016), 621-633.

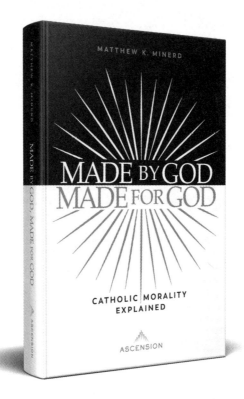

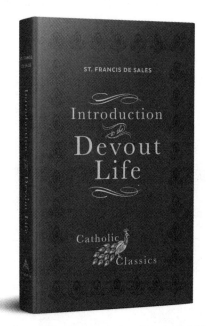

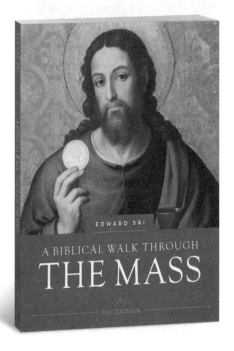